MW01223837

LOOKING FABULOUS

WITH

BEAUTY FOOD

NUTRITION TIPS, BEST HOMEMADE BEAUTY RECIPES

&

FRENCH BEAUTY SECRETS

COLETTE CECILE

Copyright © 2014 by Colette Cecile

Cover photograph copyright © Park Studio

Cover design by Fiverr.com

ISBN-13: 978-0692531723

ISBN-10: 0692531726

Published by Createspace Inc. USA

Printed by Createspace Inc. USA

All Rights Reserved

No part of this publication may be reproduced in any form or by any means, including scanning, photocopying, or otherwise without prior written permission of the copyright holder.

From the same author:

Colette Cecile, *Ces aliments qui embellissent*

Email: btfoodproject1@gmail.com

Facebook: Beauty Food Project

DEDICATION

To my parents who saw me suffering with skin problems and stimulated me to find a new path. To my grandmother who was one of my main inspirations for writing this guide. At 98, she had a gorgeous and almost wrinkle-free face. She used many of the recipes described in this book all her life. To my mom who also followed this natural beauty routine. At 88, she still has smooth and beautiful skin.

CONTENTS

FOREWORD

Looking Fabulous with Beauty Food is a fun and user-friendly book written with charm and whimsy from a French perspective. When you open this extraordinary beauty guide, you enter a new chapter in your life. The author Colette Cecile is not a supermodel, a physician or a nutritionist. She is a woman who decided one day to transform herself into a healthy, happy and radiant 50+ woman.

Colette Cecile gives you the tools to succeed. She will stimulate your appetite for delicious well-balanced meals and increase your desire for a better looking you. Discover uncomplicated solutions based on an all-inclusive diet plan with quick, simple, homemade skin care recipes for a radiant complexion. Women and men of all ages can benefit from learning these tools. It is an entertaining read that allows for making cost effective choices to attain your inner and outer beauty.

I consider *Looking Fabulous with Beauty Food* a gift. It delivers in one package all you need to know to improve your appearance from the inside out. As a health professional, I work with people on a daily basis to achieve just this approach. I recommend this one of a kind beauty guide. Use this wonderful book in your daily life. You have found your personal French beauty consultant.

Mary Jane O'Byrne, D.TCM R. Ac; Nutritional Microscopist
Health Matters Consulting
www.health-matters.ca

Acknowledgments

I would like to thank my friends, who encouraged me to share the beauty secrets in this book, beauty secrets that helped all of us. I would also like to acknowledge the people I've met who complimented my hair and complexion and asked me for beauty advice. Ultimately, they pushed me to write this guide. A special thanks to my beloved husband, who supported me through my experiments and was my guinea pig. All the anti-aging recipes work so well on his dry, mature skin!

Thank you to Evelyn King, D.D.S, Lidwine Baltenneck and Simone Grady.

Special thanks to my editors, Taylor Houghton and Ernie Cordonier.

I would like to thank Mary Jane O'Byrne, who guided me towards balanced and healthy nutrition.

DISCLAIMER

All advice and recipes found in this book are intended to inform the reader for their own personal use and not to diagnose, prescribe, treat, cure or prevent any disease. The author declines any responsibilities for all actions taken by the reader based on the information described in this book. Consult a health professional or doctor prior to any change of diet. Use caution with beauty products such as essential oils, and please keep out of reach of children. Check with your physician or dermatologist for any possibility of allergy or sensitivities to food or beauty products. Do not use the information in this guide as a substitute for medical counseling. If you have any disease that requires medical attention, seek a qualified healthcare professional.

After that, enjoy your foods as beauty enhancers!

INTRODUCTION

Stendhal, a French writer, said that beauty is a promise of happiness.

Being beautiful makes you happy. And if you're happy, your complexion will glow. How we feel internally presents itself externally. But some days, the quest for ideal beauty seems so far away. Don't worry!

Be ready to look your best for life, and consider this book as your personal beauty trainer.

I'm inviting you to explore the world of natural beauty the way you never imagined it. Success is waiting for you if you adopt a simple method based on the internal and external use of food. Improving your looks doesn't have to be tedious. You have all the elements in front of you.

This guide gives you the beauty tools to be beautiful with beauty foods.

It shows you how to:

- Eat for your beauty with the healthiest and the most delicious nutrition.

- Get glowing skin, shiny hair, and great figure with the use of low cost and highly effective products with one hundred percent active ingredients.

- Easily solve your beauty issues at home. Create in a few minutes your personalized beauty skin care. No one knows your hair and skin better than you do. Learn simple recipes that target your specific concerns and give amazing results.

- Avoid toxins from beauty products and cosmetics that could end up in your bloodstream. Why would you apply chemicals on your skin and put your health at risk?

This book is the result of years of research focusing on a beauty routine that is both natural and gentle, without compromising results. In the past, beauty products often disappointed me. I bought creams, serums, foundations, with the hope that I would find a miracle cure for my beauty concerns. The result: a collection of cosmetics that proved ineffective. I didn't know what to do!

My beauty problem? Acne. Because of this, both my self-esteem and self-confidence suffered. While living abroad, I somehow forgot about healthy nutrition and homemade beauty products, which my grandmother and my mother both utilized. I gained weight, developed cellulite on my thighs, my hair became brittle and dull, and my acne persisted. I had to find a solution! One day, during my summer vacation when visiting my parents in the south of France, I found an old and stained notebook that belonged to my grandmother. The pages were full of hand-written recipes and personal notes. There were recipes of all kinds: an avocado mask, body lotions made with oils, and food-based hair treatments. She also wrote about how to use fruit and veggies as makeup tools. My French heritage gave me the solutions I had been searching for. I just had to go back to the basics.

Despite living far away from France, I decided right away to reconnect to the French way of cooking which emphasizes the use of fresh food. I began to take more and more pleasure in creating delicious meals from scratch, knowing they would be beneficial for my health and beauty.

French people love food, and cooking remains a meaningful part of their culture. They take time to select their products to create delicious healthy dishes. They enjoy their meals sitting at the family table (not at the kitchen counter) and they eat slowly for hours while talking. Eating is a ritual. This may be their secret to the famous *joie de vivre* (joy of life).

I was motivated to come back to the healthy path my family's previous generations followed. I became addicted to a beauty-oriented diet too. I organized my life and my nutrition to regain confidence in my appearance. I opted for simple and delicious recipes, keeping in mind which foods would give me the best results in search for gorgeous skin, healthy hair, and a nice figure.

With the help of a nutritionist and information from books and reputable websites, I also learned what I could eat to eliminate the pimples that had lingered for a significant portion of my life. Gradually, my skin improved to the point of being clear. I happily decided to continue my quest and further my research.

The same summer I found my grandmother's notebook, I attended a beauty workshop where only food was used to create basic cosmetics and skin care products. Red beets, red berries, eggs, honey, and yogurt were on the instructor's desk. I was puzzled and remember thinking: am I in the wrong workshop? As it turned out, I was at the right place. The instructor explained how easily we could make effective homemade beauty products with food, just as my grandmother wrote it in her cooking/beauty book. I was blown away! The workshop prompted a new goal: to be beautiful the natural way, just like my grandmother.

I decided to use an egg white mask, a real old-fashioned recipe that my grandmother had often used. In the past, I didn't understand what she was doing when she applied this mixture on her face. After trying the recipe for myself, I was no longer left guessing; my skin was firm and glowing! I was dreaming. With one simple egg, my complexion was gorgeous.

Thrilled with the results, I continued with crazy cosmetic experiments inspired by the beauty workshop. It didn't take long before I was cutting a slice of red beet and using it as a lip tint. The color was long-lasting, and the tint didn't leave my lips sticky. Next, I dehydrated a red beet to create a powder and used it as blush. The list goes on and on. I couldn't believe the best cosmetics were coming from ingredients in my kitchen.

When someone asks me what the secret is to my complexion, the answer is simple: food.

You too can discover beauty food. Through advice offered in this guide, you're going to establish your own beauty strategy in an inexpensive, natural, and simple way! Then, you can say: *I look great: thanks to my beauty food! Refrigerator, refrigerator, tell me... Am I beautiful?*

I'm fifty-one years old and many people think I look younger, thanks to my natural beauty routine. Get ready to leave dull complexion, red itchy patches, and dark circles behind. Not only did a food-based beauty program help me improve my looks, it allowed me to take charge of my health. My nutritionist's advice also helped me to select and use beautifying foods in my daily meal preparation.

The methods in this book will give you the keys to unlock your true beauty. You'll learn the beauty secrets of French women (which they don't divulge easily), and apply them to yourself. Remember to be patient and kind to yourself. The results will come gradually, starting with subtle changes. Choose foods that are best suited to your metabolism and your needs. Study your body's response and check for any reaction (positive or negative).

Life is beauty food!

Now, let's begin.

PS: This book has been written for women (and men) from the age of 14 to 100 +: it should be savored up to the last chapter without any moderation!

CHAPTER 1

NUTRITION AND BEAUTY

WHAT IS THE BEST NUTRITION FOR BEAUTY?

There are more and more studies showing the link between nutrition and beauty. A new approach is emerging from studies and scientific research; nutritionists are calling it the skin diet. Nowadays, nutritional science gives answers and explains why and how food can make you more beautiful.

Many nutritionists are confirming that the ingestion of some specific foods can have benefits for both skin and hair. On the other hand, poor nutrition can harm your appearance and cause acne, cellulite, wrinkles, and lead to obesity.

When we are younger, the body can cope with hamburgers and pizza/pops on a regular basis without consequences (but this diet is not recommended). Once we reach a certain age, it is not the same. The turnover of the human cells slows down by the age of 30. Who didn't get a poor complexion and dark circles after a party full of excess?

So, zoom in on your plate! Know that, what you eat influences your health internally *and* externally.

If you have any health issues, you might not look your best. Your skin is a messenger of what's going on inside. Any pimples, eczema, or signs of premature aging is your body's way of calling for help. Hair and nails can also indicate if you are in good or bad health. You have the solution if you decide to follow the right nutrition and stay away from unhealthy foods.

A glowing complexion begins in the deepest parts of our body: our skin represents the visible surface of our internal cellular balance. Our epidermis protects us from exterior aggression, acts like a thermostat and helps to excrete the toxins we might have absorbed. Our skin is the mirror of our health.

The foundation for good health is rooted in your intestinal system. Proper digestion is vital to reap the benefits of your diet. Think of the saying, we are what we eat. Let's alter this saying for the sake of accuracy: we are what we absorb. If you have digestive problems or hepatic weakness, even the best nutrition will not deliver all the benefits it should.

So, let's start step by step to achieve results with beautifying foods.

Discover the logical steps of this method based on the advice from the top nutritionists in the world.

Step 1: The Health and Beauty Food Program

Your program should begin with a health assessment. Start with a simple visit to your doctor (naturopath, nutritionist, or dietitian) and ask for a blood test. Check for any vitamin or mineral deficiencies. Poor complexion, acne, or greasy hair can have a medical explanation. In my case, I was able to construct a beauty and health plan after obtaining the results of my blood tests. A weak liver, an allergy to gluten, and too much sugar in my diet were the main problems I faced. I decided to change my food choices accordingly. I underwent a detox under the supervision of my nutritionist (detoxes should always be physician-approved). After a gluten-free diet and hepatic support, my skin began to change. Thanks to healthy food, I noticed a clearer and more radiant complexion.

I know some people who are blessed with gorgeous skin, so this chapter may not captivate them. However, for many people, being beautiful requires personal effort. Remember, the key to beauty is on your plate. Take charge of yourself. Do your homework. Be your own savior.

Step 2: Hydration and Beauty

Good hydration is one of the answers to great skin and hair. Water helps maintain the body's hydric balance and plays an important role in beauty. In terms of chemical composition, skin is seventy percent water, and we need that water to keep our complexion smooth and soft. If you drink enough clear water, you can reduce and prevent wrinkles, dark circles, and large pores.

Healthcare professionals advise drinking at least 1.5 to 2 liters a day of mineral or filtered water, plus even larger quantities in summer. In this book, you'll discover great ideas to achieve the optimal hydration with herbal teas, delicious juices, and smoothies. You'll achieve your beauty goals in such a simple way. Remember to stay away from soda and carbonated beverages that are loaded with sugar and can contribute to skin problems and weight gain.

Step 3: Beauty's Bad Friends

Before going any further, you need to know the substances that are harmful to your beauty or as I call them, beauty's bad friends.

Sugar

Sugar, an enemy of your beauty? It's true. Many healthcare professionals are discovering the harmful effects of sugar. A high consumption of sugar can threaten your health in the form of diabetes and obesity. It's not surprising to learn that sugar also can have harmful effects on your beauty, causing skin to sag and wrinkle. How? When sugar enters the bloodstream, it bonds with protein molecules such as collagen and elastin; this process creates a phenomenon called glycation or AGEs (Advanced Glycation End Products). To simplify, the proteins are destroyed by sugar. Therefore, glycation reduces the production of collagen, skin's elasticity, and leads to premature aging. Acne or varicose veins can be triggered by sugar too. Modern diets are based on foods which are heat-processed, and these foods contain AGE products.

When I stopped consuming sugar on a regular basis, my skin cleared up almost entirely. Through a combination of topical treatments made with food and reducing my sugar intake, I achieved my goals: my complexion glowed and was pimple-free.

Did you know? Cancer cells thrive on sugar. Scientists say sugar encourages cancer cells to multiply faster.

So, does that mean you need to deprive yourself? No, of course not. This beauty nutrition program is designed to be fun. It goes beyond the standard meal preparation. This guide shows you how to adopt another life style and how to enjoy delicious healthy food without giving up a happy life.

So, let's find a natural solution for your sweet cravings. Stevia, which scores zero on the glycemic index, is a plant which is three hundred times sweeter in its powder form than table sugar. It has been used for centuries in Japan and South America. Xylitol is another great alternative and scores a seven on the glycemic index. It's extracted from corncobs and hardwood such as birch. Coconut sugar, which scores thirty-five on the glycemic index is a healthier choice than regular sugar which scores sixty. You can purchase them in health food stores.

I have used stevia and xylitol in all my desserts since my nutritionist advised me to do so. Guess what? My family and friends don't notice a difference. Eliminating sugar doesn't mean you can't indulge.

Refined Flour

An excessive intake of white bleached flour increases the glycemic level in the bloodstream; more insulin must be produced, promoting the storage of fat. This imbalance leads to weight gain and heart disease. White flour is not a friend of your health or your beauty. It's called "glue of the gut". Think of it this way: flour and water make an amazing glue, great for crafts, not so great for digestion. Remember the first rule for good health is digestion.

Refined flours contain chemical residue and don't offer any nutritional benefit because the outside bran layer and the germ are missing. Refined flours are highly acidic, stimulate chronic inflammation, and cause numerous health issues. Of course, any internal problem will show on your skin. That's why nutritionists advise using whole wheat flour such as spelt flour, which contains more fiber. There are gluten-free flours that can be a healthy substitute for white flour. Some examples are brown rice flour, coconut flour, amaranth flour, almond flour or hazelnut flour. These flours are great while combined with tapioca or potato starch. White pasta should also be replaced with whole grain pasta.

Preservatives and Food Additives

Preservatives are used to prevent food spoilage and allow a longer shelf life. Some common preservatives include ascorbic acid, sulfur dioxide, and sulfite. Food additives are used in foods to change the color and taste. Sugar, monosodium glutamate (MSG), trans-fat, coloring agents, and aluminum are all examples of food additives. You'll find these *bad friends* in pre-packaged food, ready-to-eat meals, and condiments. They disturb our metabolism at the cellular level.

Wine contains sulfates but it also has polyphenols (antioxidants), which are great for anti-aging prevention. Switching to organic wine is even better.

Hydrogenated Fats or Trans-fats

Trans-fats are created when oil is heated. Hydrogenated fats are added to packaged food and fast food to extend their shelf lives. Nutritionists call this dead food. Trans-fats bombard our cells with an excess of free radicals and this leads to premature aging. These hydrogenated fats are known to cause cancer, heart disease, and chronic inflammation because the body becomes less able to defend itself at the cellular level. Foods with trans-fats have no fresh nutritious elements. So, take the time to prepare a real meal with real food! My nutritionist gave me another piece of advice: eliminate canned food that contains Bisphenol-A (BPA) from my diet.

Did you know? Countries where people don't consume dead food have virtually no problems with acne or eczema!

Try your best to avoid these enemies of your beauty. Read product labels. If you see trans-fat, choose something else. I know it may seem daunting; how can you live without pizza, cookies, and so on? So, indulge yourself and try first to reduce your intake of dead food. Replace them with great alternatives and soon, your body won't have cravings for bad food anymore.

Think about all the consequences if you follow a poor diet (weight gain, cellulite, acne, and wrinkles). It will help you to stay on the right path.

You also need to pay attention to acid-forming food. Try to get a pH test from your local health food store. It will tell you if you must emphasize on alkaline foods such as fruit, veggies, and grains; reduce your intake of meats, coffee and processed foods. Say goodbye to your beauty if you want to fool around with bad food!

The final enemies to your beauty will be no surprise: excessive consumption of alcohol (dry out your skin), smoking (no rosy complexion if you smoke), prolonged sun exposure (skin aging/brown spots) and stress, all of which have detrimental effects to both your internal and external health.

Step 4: Little Changes for Big Results

You want results in your quest for beauty, right? Be ready for a little facelift of your kitchen! I'm not speaking of physical renovations, but rather making some healthy changes when stocking your pantry and refrigerator. Discover a French attitude towards food. You'll love preparing meals the way French people do. Think about your food as beauty tools to build your own beauty plan.

Here are some suggestions:

- Gradually eliminate canned foods and other prepackaged foods (dead foods vs. fresh beauty foods). They are a downer for your beauty! Choose fresh, organic or local food. If you don't have time, frozen fruit or veggies are a great alternative. In France, people do not have a big pantry to accumulate nonperishable items: they prefer to get fresh food to cook. Go to the farmer's market as much as possible. In France, it is a tradition to go to the market and select the best quality items that you can find from each merchant. These local markets may be tourist attractions for foreigners but for Europeans, they are the key to great nutrition. You might also go to health food stores which offer wonderful local produce all year around.

- Avoid frying food with oils at high temperatures: you'll end up with free radicals on your plate and negative cellular changes in your body (which means health issues, wrinkles, and premature aging). You must find the time to get your beautifying foods on a regular basis. If you have no time, appoint somebody to do it for you (a friend or an available family member).

- Eat quietly with no TV on. Listen to music you love and enjoy your meal with pleasure and peace. Stimulate your palate with colorful and tasty dishes.

Think of food as your beauty friend and not as your enemy. You will look good, feel happy and be successful in your private life and work... and age well!

Here are more tips:

- Add a gorgeous and colorful palette to your kitchen counters with fresh, local or organic fruit. Most French kitchens display food everywhere (woven garlic, tomatoes on a plate, ripe fruit) that stimulate your senses. You will be delighted to see your new beauty friends asking to be picked and savored! Your fridge also should get a load of crispy salads and amazing veggies.

- Buy a lovely glass container or pot and fill it with natural dried fruit (your new healthy candies). Display in a glass jar high fiber pasta (whole grain pasta). If you see on a regular basis colorful pasta, like spinach pasta, you will use them in your meals. Be like an interior decorator and beautify your kitchen with healthy ingredients.

- Adopt one of these healthiest ways of cooking (or all of them):

  - **Steaming**: You will keep all the nutrients you need for your beauty program.

  - **Stir-frying**: Invest in a wok; you will never regret it.

  - **Broiling**: This healthy way of cooking (dry-heat) requires marinating meat beforehand.

  - **Slow cooking:** Discover new recipes and try to do a delicious beef stew. You will understand why French recipes such as *boeuf bourguignon* or *blanquette de veau* (despite the rich wine-cream sauce) are typical dishes which don't make you gain weight. You can find these two great recipes at www.foodnetwork.com. For making the sauce, you can replace heavy cream with unsweetened coconut milk. Reduce barbecuing: French people don't often use BBQ to cook (only in summer with friends for a party on the patio or in the garden). This method is not the best for your beauty. Some experts in nutrition denounce the formation of Advanced Glycation End Products (or AGEs) which occurs when animal-derived foods are cooked at very high temperature. The World Health Organization for Research on Cancer declared that barbecued meat may create carcinogenic compounds which have shown causing cancers in animal studies. These AGEs may contribute to formation of inflammation and can be a factor to health issues and premature aging. So, marinate meat beforehand to reduce risk.

- When you have time, bake delicious cookies and cakes (yummy) with these new ingredients (stevia, xylitol, coconut sugar, and gluten-free flour) we talked about earlier. Serve cookies on a gorgeous tray and enjoy them alone or with your family and friends. Bring some healthy cookies to your work place (as well as trail mix and baby carrots or fresh apple wedges). You will be the envy of your colleagues! Wait to see their reaction to your improved looks.

- Use Himalayan salt. My nutritionist introduced me to this pink Himalayan salt; it's healthy and full of minerals.

- Switch from milk chocolate to dark chocolate.

- Switch from white rice to brown rice or quinoa. Replace your regular pasta with whole-wheat pasta or gluten-free pasta.

- Reduce your intake of coffee and discover the refreshing and beautiful world of green teas or herbal teas. Nutritionists say that coffee is a burden on your adrenal glands and liver.

THE A-LIST BEAUTY FOOD

How Food Can Make You Beautiful

Now you know, beauty begins on your plate. Your meal represents your first beauty step before skin care and cosmetics. The beautifying foods contain vitamins and minerals that work from the inside out. Therefore, they are essential to you. Fill your body with beauty-fuel ingredients. You'll be energized, and it will show on your skin and hair too.

Of course, nutritional supplements can help in case of deficiencies. However, some nutritionists and dietitians doubt the total effectiveness of these pills. In fact, some studies show that capsules or tablets aren't always well absorbed by the intestinal system. Before all, the intestinal flora must be in good shape.

Did you know? Sometimes, supplementation is needed. For example, you might have to take digestive enzymes for better digestion. Talk about it with your naturopath.

My nutritionist recommends that I take probiotics too. Probiotics help the intestinal tract to absorb vitamins and minerals from food. There are natural probiotics in yogurt, kefir, and fermented cabbage.

Great nutrition is the right answer. The solution is in your kitchen!

One more time, your target is to concentrate on your beauty food.

A study revealed that, in two groups of women comprised of all ages, the group who ate lots of fruit and veggies showed a more radiant and supple complexion than the other group who had poor nutrition and took supplements.

Here is the list of the principal vitamins and minerals you can get from beautifying foods:

- **Vitamin A** plays an essential role in the growth of epidermal cells. It fights against skin aging, protects from UV rays, increases collagen production, and improves skin quality in both thickness and elasticity. The carotenoids (colored pigments) help fight against free radicals. You've probably heard of Beta-carotene; in the body, it is transformed to pro-vitamin A. Food containing this precious vitamin will give you a glowing complexion and will prevent your skin from becoming dry. Be careful: an excess of vitamin A is toxic. Please consult with your doctor before trying anything.

- **Vitamin B** helps repair collagen fibers and elastin (biotin, for example, is essential for nails and hair).

- **Vitamin C** needs to be obtained through nutrition as much as possible. Our body doesn't produce or store vitamin C. This vitamin restores skin's elasticity.

- **Vitamin E** is the first line of defense against cell oxidation. It helps fight exterior aggressions and maintains the softness and elasticity of the skin.

- **Zinc** is an essential mineral for healthy skin, great hair, and nails. It's ideal to fight against skin problems such as acne and eczema. This trace mineral is very important for the synthesis of proteins and cell division.

- **Selenium**, in conjunction with vitamin E and Zinc, does wonders for hair and nails. It's also an anti-aging mineral.

- **Iron** deficiencies give you a greyish complexion. Be careful: iron is very oxidizing. That's why it's better to get it from food than from supplements. Always check with your doctor to see if you have iron deficiencies.

- **Sulfur** is known as *the* beauty mineral. It's found in keratin. This fibrous protein helps nails stay strong. It's necessary to produce collagen.

Other important components:

- **Omega-3s** are a type of good fat that ensures your cells stay hydrated.

- **Proteins** stimulate keratin formation that benefits skin, hair, and nails.

Now, discover or rediscover the magical foods. You are a step closer to looking great!

In the next section, you will find a list of food followed by the letter A (for vitamin A) or C (for vitamin C) etc. It will indicate the major vitamins found in veggies or fruit (to help you make the best selection).

These are guidelines and tips advised by the best nutritionists including my nutritionist. You'll achieve improvements in your health and beauty goals with healthy and delicious nutrition.

Warning: before making any changes in your diet, check with your doctor for allergies to any kind of food.

Eat Your Veggies!

Your goal: five servings of veggies a day. It's a lot, but you should try to eat *all* these servings. Do you know why? To be more beautiful!

If you want a radiant complexion, you need to eat your veggies. This is an instant beauty fix. Steaming your veggies *al dente* is the healthiest way to enjoy them. Salads are amazing too; they deliver one hundred percent of their vitamins to your metabolism.

Visit farmers' markets, go to your health food stores and choose local or organic veggies. It is fun to prepare your beauty food list with fresh ingredients.

Veggies You Should Eat Frequently

- Broccoli (C)

- Green cabbage (C)

- Kale (C)

- Green Beans (K)

- Asparagus (B&C)

- Red and Green Peppers (C, more than in oranges)

- Fennel (C)

- Mushrooms (Selenium & Zinc)

Did you know? Putting a drizzle of fat like olive oil on veggies will favor a better absorption of the nutrients.

Beneficial Greens

- Spinach (C)

- Romaine Lettuce (K)

- Watercress (C)

Did you know? Nutritionists recommend eating a salad with meat. These green foods contain digestive enzymes that help you digest proteins better. One more advice: it is better to eat veggies raw or *al dente* (most of the vitamin C is depleted after they are cooked).

Carotenoids

Carotenoids are plant pigments found in fruit or veggies with bright red, orange, or yellow color. They contain pro-vitamin A that will help you to slow down the aging process (and give you a rosy complexion).

- Carrot (A&C)

- Pumpkin (A)

- Squash (A)

Seasoning Agents

- Parsley (A&C)

- Fresh Ginger (C)

- Garlic (Sulfur)

- Onion (Sulfur)

Other Vegetables

- Potatoes (A&C/Iron), when steamed or baked, are considered acceptable by nutritionists. Sorry, French fries don't belong to this list.

- Tomatoes (C), which truly belong to the fruit category, contain lycopene, a type of antioxidant. Your homemade spaghetti sauce will help you get radiant skin.

- Red Beets (C) and Raw Red Cabbage (C) are full of polyphenols, which is a precious antioxidant (found in dark chocolate).

- Avocado (E/C&A) is the king of your beauty program. Again, it's botanically a fruit. Most important, it contains *good* fat.

- Seaweed (Calcium/Magnesium) is full of minerals and proteins (vegetarian option). It can be used fresh or dehydrated. Here are a few types of seaweed: agar-agar, dulse, nori, iziki, and wakame. Micro algae, such as spirulina and chlorella, can be great additions to smoothies.

Eat Your Fruit!

Just like veggies, you need five servings of fruit a day. It adds color to your plate and is a natural way to fulfill your cravings for something sweet. It also offers a variety of vitamins and antioxidants. Radiant skin and shiny hair are a product of consuming the right fruit. Fruit is your ally in maintaining skin elasticity and youthful appearance; it can rejuvenate your skin by stimulating cell renewal. Fruit plays a fundamental role in maintaining fresh and glowing look.

You'll find below a list of beauty fruit organized by color. Let's focus on the nutrients fruit offers you:

- **Red:** strawberries (C), cherries (C), raspberries (C), grape (C), watermelon (A). They contain lycopene (as in tomato), a powerful antioxidant.

- **Yellow:** banana (A&B), peach (A&B), apple (B), pear (B), pineapple (C).

- **Orange:** orange (C), mandarin (C), grapefruit (C), apricot (A), mango (C&A), papaya (C), guava (C, more than in kiwi), melon (C).

- **Purple:** plums (A&K), red grapes (B/Polyphenols), blueberries (C&E), black currants (C&E). These fruit fight against the cell aging process.

- **Green:** pear (B), white grapes (C&B), kiwi (C, more than in oranges), apple (C/Flavonoids-a powerful antioxidant).

Did you know? Nutritionists recommend eating fruit between meals or at least 30 minutes before meal.

A blind study, conducted in multiple countries, showed that women who consumed fruit daily had a more radiant skin than women who didn't. The most convincing evidence? The photos taken throughout the study.

So, adopt the beauty food attitude and take pictures of yourself! A real makeover from the inside out! See the before and after shot. By the way, you might lose weight too.

Tip: make your own marmalade sweetened with stevia, xylitol, or coconut sugar and add agar-agar as a gelling agent (substitute to gelatin). Homemade applesauce (or red berries compote) is another handy ingredient. French people use it in baking as a sweetener in their baking recipes or with granola at breakfast.

Eat Your "Good" Fats!

What? Nutritionists want you to eat fats?
Fats from whole foods bring energy to your body, allow great absorption of vitamins, and play a vital role for your health. Good fats can even help you to lose weight. How? Good fats incorporated in your diet will stimulate the feeling of being full.

And what about beauty? Those good fats moisturize and lubricate your epidermis from the inside. Without them, your skin wouldn't be supple and elastic. As I promised you, this method is not synonymous with deprivation. It's based on customizing your food choices for your health and beauty needs. You can have things like butter (which contains vitamin A) in moderation. If possible, choose organic hormone-free butter. Goat milk butter is my favorite.

Oleaginous fruit represents a great source of beauty fat and antioxidants. So, on a daily basis, enjoy avocado and nuts. Adding nuts to your salad not only give the dish more texture, it allows for a beneficial combination of vitamin C and vitamin E.

Your health and your beauty need a diet with fatty acids (FAs). Essential fatty acids (EFAs) can't be synthesized by the body, that's why you should get them through your food. It's a win-win situation for your hair, nails, and your anti-aging strategy! These EFAs are necessary for good function of body tissue; they are in the membranes of every cell and regulate inflammatory processes. Deficiencies in fatty acids can lead to health issues, dry skin, and acne. Fatty acids added to your diet will help you to keep your skin firm and well lubricated.

The most important factor is to get them in a proper ratio: the best ratio of omega-6 to omega-3 is 4:1. In Western diets, the ratio is 15:1, sometimes even as high as 20:1. The consequences of this imbalance are inflammatory and autoimmune diseases, cancer, and cardiovascular disease.

The modern diet relies on processed and packaged food that contains dangerous trans-fats. We get too much omega-6s compared to omega-3s, meaning not enough seafood, nuts, and seeds. Achieving the right balance isn't always easy. Both omega-3s and omega-6s play an essential role in hair growth and skin health but you should keep in mind that some omega-6s might stimulate inflammation in your cells.

Eat cold-water fish and avocados. Use unrefined cold pressed oils in dressings or while cooking. This will help your skin whether you're fighting acne or trying to deter the aging process.

Let's get technical about omega-3s, 6s and 9s.
Omega-3s and **Omega-6s** are polyunsaturated fats and called essential fatty acids or EFAs. The body can't produce them; they

must be obtained through your diet or supplementation. Omega-3s contain EPA (elcosapentaenoic acid), DHA (docosahexaenoic acid), and ALA (alpha-linoleic acid). GLA (gamma-linolenic acid) belongs to the omega-6s category, and can be found in black currant seed oil, evening primrose oil, and borage oil. Check with your doctor or naturopath before using these oils.

Omega-9s are monounsaturated fats and called non-essential. Supplementation is not necessary. The main type of omega-9 is oleic acid found in olive oil, sunflower oil, nuts, seeds, and animal fat.

So, enjoy these oils internally, and topically once you get to the next chapters regarding external use.

Extra virgin cold pressed olive oil is an excellent choice. It has a balanced ratio of omega-3s and omega-6s at 1:1 and contains omega-9s too. You need to buy the best quality olive oil you can find to reap all its benefits.

You must learn which oil to use for deep-frying to avoid getting trans-fats on your plate. Choose the one with a high smoke point. Some nutritionist's advice is to use coconut oil; others prefer olive oil or grape seed oil. You can play with other oils listed below. Use them in your salad dressing, add them to your smoothies, and put a touch of oil on your veggies.
Here are some animal and plant sources of omega fatty acids:

- **Omega-3**: eggs, pumpkin seeds, walnuts, walnut oil, canola oil, hemp seed oil, ground flax seeds, flax seed oil, chia seeds, spirulina, green leafy vegetables (watercress sprouts, Brussels's sprouts, and spinach), seafood, shrimp, sardines, herring, mackerel, wild chinook or sockeye salmon, anchovies.

- **Omega-6**: eggs, Brazil nuts, pecan nuts, cashew nuts, olive oil, grape seed oil, sesame oil, evening primrose oil, borage oil, sunflower oil.

- **Omega-9**: avocados, almonds, hazelnuts, macadamia nuts, olive oil.

You should eat fish two or three times a week to get your omega-3s. Try steaming it. If you can't eat fish on regular basis, ask your naturopath about omega-3s supplementation.

Eat Your Proteins!

Skin, hair, and nails as well as eyes and muscles, are made of keratin. This protein protects us from exterior aggressors and gives our bodies structure. It gives sheen to the skin and plumps out fines lines. Collagen is also a fibrous protein that holds together cells. Loss of collagen means wrinkles, sagging skin, and lack of skin firmness.

Nutritionists advise choosing a good source of protein in your daily meal preparation if you want to prevent and smooth out lines. Depending on your age, your activity level, your health and weight, your protein intake may vary. Trust your body and listen to what it's telling you. In general, the recommended daily intake is 56 grams. It's wise to meet a nutritionist, and calculate your protein ratio adapted to your needs.

Best Source of Plant-Based Proteins

- Mushroom

- Seaweed

- Spinach

- Kale

- Broccoli

- Cauliflower

- Brown rice

- Quinoa

- Lentils

- Chickpeas

- Dried legumes (beans)

Best Source of Animal-Derived Proteins

- Shrimps

- Oysters

- Egg yolk

- Small fishes: sardines, anchovies, mackerel, trout

- Wild salmon

- Grass fed organic beef, particularly lean cuts

- Organic free-range chicken, organic free-range turkey

- Milk, cheese, and yogurt contain proteins too, as well as calcium for your bones and teeth

One forgotten source of protein is preparing your own beef or chicken broth with meat and bones. This provides a wonderful base for soups. You can find tutorials if you're unfamiliar with making stock. This type of broth is still used by lots of French chefs because it's full of flavor. Knowing you can get collagen back into your skin (thanks to a broth) makes you smile, but why not to begin your anti-aging plan with this?

You will find a great combination of proteins and essential fats when you eat the small fishes mentioned earlier 2 times per week (it belongs to the Mediterranean Diet as well as tomatoes and olives). Salmon and avocado should also be consumed once or twice a week. If you're looking for a boost of vitamin E, drizzle wheat germ oil over your pasta or steamed veggies.

Don't forget to add herbs and spices to your dishes; they allow you to create great variations and add flavor.

Herbs and Spices

- Fennel

- Cinnamon

- Parsley

- Ginger

- Turmeric

- Basil

- Oregano

Tip: enjoy dry grated coconut which is full of trace minerals such as iron, zinc, copper, and manganese. Incorporated in smoothies or desserts, it will give your skin, hair, and nails a boost.

NUTRITION TIPS TO FIGHT SOME BEAUTY PROBLEMS

Every skin type requires specific skin care, right?

The same way, every skin type may require a specific nutrition.

Again, check with your doctor if you have an allergy to specific food or if you take medication. You want to rule out reactions and interactions.

Dietitians say that for every skin problem, you have your vegetable or fruit to solve it!

You will find health and beauty solutions with the right foods and plants, but don't forget this: a proper amount of sleep, exercise, hydration, no smoking and little alcohol will help you beyond your expectations!

Nutrition Tips to Fight Acne & Oily Skin

Did you know that acne could disappear with a good diet? There's a book devoted to explaining how, it is called *The Clear Skin Diet* by Alan C. Logan. Once I switched to an anti-acne diet with the guidance of my nutritionist, my skin improved immensely. This new strategy helped also other friends to clear their skin. If they get a pimple, they know the cause: they weren't eating the right foods!

Prepare your meals with specific ingredients...

Anti-Acne Diet

- Gluten-free bread

- Artichokes

- Parsley

- Broccoli

- Fennel

- Stinging nettle plant

- Celery

- Cucumber

- Carrots

- Spinach

- Red pepper

- Garlic

- Lettuce

- Radish

- Apple

- Apricot

Snacks Suggestions

- Almonds

- Slices of apple dipped in almond butter

- Celery sticks dipped in unsweetened goat's milk yogurt

Tip: dairy can be a trigger for acne. Some alternatives are almond or coconut milk, and soy milk.

Anti-Acne Drinks

First, you need to drink lots of fluids to help eliminate pimples. Mineral water or filtered water is your friend. Goodbye sodas and other sweeten beverages.

Herbal teas are another drink that keeps acne at bay. Sage, thyme, peppermint, and green tea prove most effective.

Do you want a beverage that's beneficial for your skin? Drink unsweetened fresh lemonade daily for its detoxifying effects. This is amazing for your complexion!

Acne Fighter Smoothie

Smoothies are effective for acne treatment because you can combine the benefits of fruit and veggies.

Blend 1 glass of unsweetened coconut milk or almond milk with 1 glass of mango slices, ½ glass of red berries and ½ glass of spinach. So tasty!

Tip: to calm down inflammation in your metabolism, eat fish (steamed) 2 or 3 times a week (if you can't eat fish on regular basis, ask your naturopath about omega-3s supplementation). If you want to eat meat, choose grass-fed and hormone-free meat.

Food to avoid

- Sugar (use instead stevia or xylitol)

- Commercial cookies

- Citrus fruit (orange, grapefruit)

- Heavy spicy food

- Cow's milk and yogurt (almond or coconut milk are the best options)

Did you know? Some people are sensitive to seafood and seaweed which can activate an acne flare up.

Nutrition Tips to Fight Greyish Complexion

A greyish complexion might be a sign of anemia (deficiency of iron). If you need to add some rosy color to your cheeks, indulge yourself with food full of vitamins. Don't forget your intake of protein too.

A smoothie is a great way to get radiant skin. Here are the best ingredients you can use:

- Strawberries

- Black currants

- Tomatoes

- Cantaloupes

- Mangoes

- Fennel

- Raw cocoa

Nutrition Tips to Fight Wrinkles and Aging Skin

Many studies show that diets rich in antioxidants, vitamin C, zinc, and good fats can help you fight free radicals that destroy collagen (less collagen=wrinkles, aging skin, and loss of elasticity). Before we get to nutrition, you need to eliminate your exposure to free radicals outside of food. This means no baking in the sun or smoking. Anti-aging food contains nutrients and vitamins that will give you incredible results.

Smoothies and juices are the key in your beauty food diet. You can create your own cocktail. Choose fruit and veggies that are full of vitamins to boost your skin from the inside and plump your complexion with an incredible glow.

Anti-Wrinkle Smoothie

Mix 1 glass of almond milk, hemp or flaxseed milk with ¼ glass of fine powdered green tea. Add 1 glass of mixed strawberries and blueberries. Delicious!

Anti-Aging Juice

With your juicer, juice the seeds of 1 pomegranate (without the white membrane), 1 apple, 2 carrots, 1 handful of kale, and 1 cup of blueberries. It is a real beauty fix!

Anti-Aging Teas

French people like to sip their special beauty herbal teas on a regular basis (here is another French beauty secret). Some specialized stores prepare cocktail of teas for beauty needs (or health issues). It is a French way of achieving beauty from the inside out.

Here are some suggestions:

- Green tea

- Hibiscus tea

- Rosehip tea (full of vitamin C). To get this one, go online or check at your health food store or tea store. Many people (including my family and me) swear by this wonderful tea and use it as a wrinkle fighter

- Stinging nettles tea (see your herbalist)

- Dandelion roots tea (see your herbalist)

Anti-Aging Diet

Nutritionists and doctors frequently advise eating foods that contain polyphenols (their molecular action is 2 times more efficient than vitamins). Scientific studies confirm that polyphenols are the best wrinkle fighters.

Following is a list of foods that are your friends to fight wrinkles:

- Strawberries
- Raspberries
- Blueberries
- Cherries
- Pomegranate
- Grapes
- Rhubarb
- Kiwi
- Mushrooms
- Carrot
- Squash
- Avocado
- Eggs
- Garlic
- Chicken liver
- Seafood

Who said that a beauty diet would be boring? You can enjoy a wide variety of foods. Just select them well and adopt a healthy way of cooking them (steamed, poached, stir-fry). Add to your diet lots of veggies (green leafy ones) and fruit.

I often meet women at the farmers' market, who are over seventy years old that have hardly any wrinkles. These women are passionate about their fruit and veggies. For me, they are a true example of the link between beauty and nutrition.

The last but certainly not the least important rule to keep in mind for anti-aging is to minimize your sugar intake.

Nutrition Tips to Fight Dry Skin

Dry skin is skin that needs hydration. So, drink water and great herbal teas. Dry skin is deprived of lipids.

You can obtain these lipids in a diet full of foods from the following list:

- Fish (sardine, wild salmon)

- Seafood

- Walnuts

- Almonds

- Red cabbage

- Green peas

- Mango

Anti-Dry Skin Smoothie

Blend 1 glass of raspberries with ¾ glass of pineapple slices and 1 avocado (ripe). Enjoy!

If you follow a low-fat diet to lose weight, you will end up with dry skin. Don't forget your omega-3s to lubricate your skin!

Nutrition Tips to Fight Brittle Hair and Nails

Your skin, hair, and nails are a mirror of your health, your nutrition, and even your emotions. Do you want to show off your shiny hair and strong nails?

Here are some foods to target those areas:

- Complete cereals

- Eggs

- Meat

- Fish

- Lentils

- Green beans

- Carrots

- Bananas

- Papayas

- Prunes

- Blueberries

- Almonds

- Walnuts

My nutritionist always advocates incorporating chlorophyll in my daily diet. It can be obtained through green veggies such as broccoli, spinach and spirulina (in powder for smoothies). Your hair and nails will be healthier!

Smoothie

Blend 1 ripe banana with 5 strawberries. Add 1 glass of oat milk and ½ glass of water.

Drinks

- Water

- Rosemary tea

- Stinging nettle tea

Nutrition Tips to Fight Hair Loss

This problem needs to be medically evaluated to determine the cause. Hormone imbalances in menopause or pregnancy can be possible causes. There is also seasonal hair loss, but this is temporary.

Nutrients to Fight Hair Loss

- Vitamin B^8 in bananas and tomatoes

- Sulfur in garlic, onions, oysters, and shrimp

- Selenium in crab meat and mussels

Did you know? Dark chocolate and raw cocoa powder may help you. Nutritionists promote it for its high content of flavonoid polyphenols. So, be a chocoholic. Your hair will thank you.

Anti-Hair Loss Drinks

- Green tea

- Peppermint tea contains anti-androgenic agents which inhibit production of dihydrotestosterone (DHT); DHT is a compound that promotes hair loss

- Rosemary tea

- Juice of carrots, spinach, and cucumber (prepare a delicious cocktail with your juicer)

Anti-Hair Loss Smoothie

Mix 1 glass of coconut milk with 1 ripe banana. Add some pumpkin seeds, ½ tsp. of spirulina, and 1 tsp. of raw cocoa powder. Sweeten with stevia or xylitol.

Nutrition Tips to Fight Cellulite and Help Weight Loss

Cellulite is often the result of bad diet and sedentary life style but can be also caused by hormone imbalance or poor blood circulation.

How to Fight Cellulite

- Move! Practice sports that target the areas plagued by cellulite. Bicycle exercise is simply the best! YouTube is a great place to look for new exercises.

- Drink lots of fluids!

- Choose drinks that stimulate your blood circulation and help eliminate toxins. The best drinks are green tea, unsweetened lemonade, and 1 tsp. of non-pasteurized apple cider in a glass of water every morning.

Juices or smoothies fill your stomach with the right ingredients. This is a delicious way to fight cellulite or to help you in a weight loss program.

Anti-Cellulite Smoothie

Here are great ingredients that will help blood flow and reduce fat!

Mix ¼ of a pineapple with ¼ cup of black grapes and ¼ cup of raspberries. It doesn't get more delicious than that.

Anti-Cellulite Juice

Mix the juice of 1 lemon with 2 kiwis and 2 pineapple slices. Add green tea prepared in advance for added weight loss benefits.

Anti-Cellulite Food

Discover your best allies when fighting cellulite or trying to lose weight:

- Asparagus
- Fennel
- Radish
- Garlic
- Spinach
- Watercress
- String beans
- Apples
- Pineapple
- Strawberries
- Papaya
- Grapefruit
- Lean white meat
- Eggs

Tip: between meals, enjoy a fruit salad with papaya and pineapple (delicious and no guilt).

Snacks

Always try to snack healthy. Here are some ideas:

- Organic baby carrots or celery sticks dipped in low-fat cottage cheese mixed with chives

- Apple wedges

- Almonds

- Pineapple slices

Did you know? Coffee doesn't play any role in your fight against cellulite or weight. However, by using coffee externally, you can fight cellulite. We'll get to this later in the book.

Weight Loss Nutrition

A weight loss diet is not about depriving yourself! You can still eat well just with some slight alterations. First, try to reduce your portion sizes. Eat a portion size equivalent to what you can hold in your hand. Your nutrition should be based on fresh food as much as possible and do your best to avoid the bad friends of beauty.

Soups, salads with protein, and smoothies are a great place to start. You can indulge yourself occasionally but don't overdo it! If you combine healthy nutrition with physical activity, you will be on the path of a new life that will lead to a new you.

Here are some reasons why French women stay thin:

- They don't eat more than they need, which is another way of saying they are reasonable with their portion sizes.

- They walk a lot. In cities finding a parking spot can be difficult, so walking is a hassle-free option. This can be inconvenient at times, but it's wonderful for the waistline.

- They take the stairs, not elevators, because often old heritage buildings don't have elevators.

Choose meals that coincide with your beauty plan. Below are some tips to keep in mind when trying to lose weight:

- Salads are great for any weight loss program. Adding the right proteins like smoked salmon, white meat, or hard-boiled eggs, turns a salad into a complete meal.

- Cinnamon, ginger, cayenne, and garlic are all seasonings that can help in your weight loss plan.

- The American journal of Clinical Nutrition claims that matcha tea can help individuals lose weight. It increases energy levels and burns fat.

- Choose light desserts like applesauce with some almonds or dark chocolate.

All these suggestions will serve you to shed extra pounds. Be patient. Changes occur gradually but require consistency for maximum effect. By eating well, your skin will glow, and your figure will follow.

RECIPES WITH BEAUTIFYING FOODS

Now, you have an idea what healthy and beautifying nutrition means. You'll notice that some foods are mentioned repeatedly; these will become part of your daily life.

Beauty foods make you look good and feel good!

Don't feel overwhelmed by these dietary changes. Adopt new foods or new menu ideas gradually. One alteration per week is a good pace to incorporate these changes.

You can also find inspiration from books and blogs. If you find yourself struggling to stick to your plan, search for a new recipe. Don't give up! Be surrounded only by beauty food.

Tip: sugar and beauty don't get along well. As a reminder, create a list for your kitchen of the glycemic index of major foods (you will find this list on-line, print it and stick it on your refrigerator). Every day, check that you eat the food at the bottom of the low glycemic index.

Drinks

- **Water** is your biggest ally. Filtered water is a safe choice.

- **Water with lemon** should be available all the time. If you like to sweeten it, use stevia or xylitol. It should be your first drink in the morning (unsweetened, cold or hot). A glowing clear complexion is waiting for you.

- **Coconut water** is becoming more and more popular. It's full of minerals, making it perfect before and after physical activity. Drink the unsweetened type.

- **Rosehip tea** not only contains anti-aging properties, it's full of vitamin C too. Check for rosehip tea at your local health food store.

- **Herbal teas** can also help you control some esthetic problems like acne or simply detoxify your metabolism gently. Seek medical advice if you take medicines that are contra-indicated with some herbal teas.

- **Organic red wine** in moderation is a great option to obtain polyphenols.

- **Fresh fruit and veggie juices** are necessary for your skin, hair, and nails. You should consider buying a juicer to create the perfect customized blend of juices that align with your beauty needs. Day by day your complexion will become more radiant, smooth, and clear. If you go to juice bars, enjoy beauty drinks that contain no sweeteners added. I juice a red beet and carrot daily (rosy cheeks guaranteed). Some of my favorite juices include orange, papaya, and guava. They are delicious and an effective combination to fight wrinkles.

- **Smoothies** are amazing for your beauty. They allow you to drink your veggies and fruit. Again, nutritionists consider smoothies a perfect option for getting all your nutrients into your metabolism quickly. Try to switch your regular milk for coconut milk, almond milk, or hemp milk. Choose fruit and vegetables suited to your beauty needs. There are countless recipes online or you can buy a book on the subject.

Now, are you ready to rediscover your meals? You can revise your regular dishes with the use of beauty food and create new dishes. It's fun and so rewarding!

Use recipes that ask for veggies (raw, steamed, or grilled in the oven) like veggie quiches. For dessert, a fruit pie is a great choice. Sometimes, just a few simple ingredients become the best meal you can imagine! Don't forget to use the right combination of foods. For example, it is better to eat meat with steamed veggies (rather than French fries) or to enjoy fruit only between meals.

Visualize your skin, hair, and figure the way you'd like them to look. Take charge of your own beauty in your kitchen!

Something magical will happen: the more veggies you eat, the more your body will crave them. Your body will become adapted to healthy food. Simple.

Part ways with sugar. Don't worry; with the help of stevia, xylitol, or coconut sugar, you will learn how to survive. Other sugar addicted people, myself included, went through a time of adaptation. It was tough, at first, but I never went back to my old diet. Your body won't need unhealthy food anymore. When you begin to see the results on your skin, hair, and figure, you'll decide to persevere with your beauty nutrition. Believe me, this is the best victory of all.

Get ready to receive compliments about your looks! If you follow this healthy nutrition based on beautifying foods, you will see the difference in the mirror and notice the way people will look at you.

Now, let's begin a beautiful day with a beauty food diet.

Breakfast

It's no surprise that nutritionists recommend starting the day with a breakfast full of healthy proteins. The main reason is that by consuming protein in the morning, it will help sustain you until lunch. If you eat sweets in the morning, you'll end up having sweet cravings all day.

Here are some suggestions:

- A slice of bread (whole wheat or gluten free) with whatever you'd like from the healthy food list. I like 1 boiled egg, radishes, one slice of bread with smoked salmon, and almond butter on a second slice.

- Yogurt and oats topped with fresh berries.

- An omelet with veggies and protein like smoked salmon.

- Homemade muffins. Carrot muffins are a great choice; just add grated carrots to your regular recipe. Use gluten-free flour and sweeten with stevia or xylitol.

- A smoothie can be the answer for you if you're in a hurry. Customize your smoothie to your desires and beauty needs. Some healthy ingredients you can include are coconut milk, almond milk, hemp seeds, dehydrated coconut fat, fresh berries, spirulina, cinnamon, or coconut water.

When it comes to drinks, get rid of your coffee and switch to green tea or herbal teas.

Fresh orange or carrot juices are wonderful for quick vitamin intake.

If you can't resist plunging into marmalade, make your own jams in the summer with wonderful red berries and enjoy them all year around. Replace sugar with stevia or xylitol and use agar-agar to jellify.

Re-think your breakfast for the sake of your health and beauty.

Lunch

If you're at work, consider a mixed salad with chicken or steamed veggies with grass-fed meat. If you are vegetarian, whole grain pasta with veggies is a good choice.

Getting results on your face and body requires an intake of healthy food daily.

If you are at home, use your imagination; create easy and healthy meals with ingredients from the beautifying diet.

Lunch suggestions for optimal beauty:

- Meat + green salad (with the beauty vinaigrette that you'll learn shortly) + steamed veggies or mashed carrots and a touch of butter.

- A rich and delicious salad with baby spinach or watercress + hard-boiled eggs + walnuts + red onion.

- Endive, lettuce, or spring mix salads + walnuts + pumpkin seeds + raspberries + smoked salmon.

Here is a personal favorite of mine:

Almond Chicken

Take 2 chicken scallops dipped in egg mixture. Prepare some whole-wheat bread crumbs mixed with almonds and walnuts; dip the scallops in the mixture. Sauté with olive oil for 5 to 8 minutes in a pan. Serve on a salad.

Now, I am ready to reveal to you a secret recipe for the healthiest salad dressing or vinaigrette you will ever taste... If you use this beauty vinaigrette, it's going to make such a difference for your health, your beauty, and your salad! Regular salad dressings are loaded with unhealthy ingredients such as trans-fat, sugar, preservatives. This is a major step in your new beauty diet. Your salad will sing! Prepare a large amount and keep it in a bottle for everyday use.

Vinaigrette Colette

This salad dressing is very healthy and great for your beauty. It is a wonder in half an avocado. You'll like it so much that you won't revert to your regular dressings full of sugar and preservatives. The base is very simple: use 3 parts oil (olive oil with avocado oil or walnut oil) to 1 part vinegar (apple cider vinegar and red wine vinegar). Add the juice of 1 lemon (alternatively, orange juice or a different beauty juice like pomegranate) and 2 or 3 tbsp. of mustard. Then, add pepper, garlic powder, ginger powder, turmeric powder, and Himalayan salt. Shake well before use.

You must think omega-3s when preparing your meals. For example:

Trout with Steamed Veggies

Choose a fresh trout filet. Steam it or fry it. Serve with 1 or 2 carrots and zucchini cut in small cubes. Add some almonds for a healthy decoration on top of the fish.

Tip: don't forget, you can add veggies to your omelets, frittata, quiches, and pasta. This is a perfect way to add variety if you want a break from steamed veggies.

Below is my favorite recipe! I created it when I grew tired of the regular pasta with tomato sauce.

Cabbage and Spaghetti Sauce Casserole

Steam wedges of a big green cabbage. In the meantime, prepare a pasta sauce with fresh tomatoes, onions, mushrooms, and a 1 tbsp. of unsweetened coconut milk. Add grass-fed ground meat and then, mix it with the tomato sauce. Put the steamed cabbage in a dish and pour the pasta sauce over it. Sprinkle some cheese if desired. Broil for 10 minutes and bake it 15 minutes on medium heat in the oven.

Nutritionists say that lunch should be the main meal, but you can also enjoy all these lunch meal suggestions for dinner.

Now, let's talk about seaweed. Seaweeds are full of vitamins, trace minerals, and antioxidants. It may seem difficult to incorporate seaweed into your diet, but I promise it's not.

Here are some suggestions:

- Use the seaweed called nori in your omelets along with some good spices.

- Try this healthy seaweed soup with dried seaweed that's soaked ahead of time for rehydration. Cook 2 medium potatoes. Mix them in a blender with soaked seaweed. Add Himalayan salt, pepper, turmeric, and a touch of soy or almond milk.

- I love having my ready-to-go seaweed butter. Mix butter and rehydrated seaweed of your choice in a processor and voila! Spread it on crackers or bread slices, or over your fish.

Dinner

Some nutritionists have a crucial rule when it comes to dinner: your last meal of the day should be light.

Why not to come back to a hearty soup? French people love their soups at night. They called this last meal *souper* because soup is the main dish. You can prepare a batch in advance for several days. Let your imagination guide you towards the veggies you like or need for your beauty diet. My grandmother loved this recipe below and I still make it on regular basis.

Leek and Potato Soup

Steam 1 big leek cut into small pieces with 2 medium sized potatoes cut into small cubes. When cooked, put the vegetables in a pot and add broth (your homemade broth if possible) to get the right consistency. You might add ½ cup of unsweetened coconut milk for a creamy effect. Don't forget your spices. You can mix it in a blender for a *velouté* style. Add some pumpkin seeds for decoration.

Here are other suggestions that you might consider for dinner time. You will enjoy them all year around. *Bon appétit!*

Watercress Soup

Wash 3 bunches of watercress and only use the leaves. Steam them with 1 potato and 2 onions. Mix them in a processor and add turkey broth or filtered water until you get the desired thickness. Add some coconut milk for a creamy effect and garnish with smoked salmon.

Omega-3 Pizza

Make your healthy pizza from scratch (if you have time, there are plenty of healthy recipes on line) or just add a healthy topping on a frozen pizza crust. No guilt, just pleasure! Use great ingredients like anchovies, fresh sardine filets, black olives, mushrooms, red or green pepper, garlic, parsley, and of course tomato sauce.

Beauty Club Sandwich

Choose toasted gluten-free bread and delicious healthy beauty foods like shrimp or smoked salmon, sprouts, baby spinach or lettuce, eggs, avocado, herbs. Avoid mayonnaise and spread some goat cheese on instead. You will be proud of this one!

Snacks and Desserts

Bite into any fruit or veggie for a snack!

Here are some great ideas:

Salted Snacks

- Enjoy carrots and celery sticks with hummus or goat milk cheese mixed with chives and walnuts.

- You can also prepare in advance your own garlic butter. Mix organic butter, garlic, salt, spices and fresh parsley. Spread on gluten free crackers.

- Have you ever tried to do a seaweed tapenade? You will need 5 little pickles, 1 tbsp. of capers, 5 tbsp. of dried seaweed and 2 shallots. Mix all the ingredients. Let marinate for several hours in 5 or 6 tbsp. of olive oil.

Sweet Snacks

- Indulge yourself with natural sugar free dried fruit. They are your new candies! A great trail mix like dried raisins, cashew nuts, almonds, dried strawberries, and apricots are wonderful when you are on the go.

- My favorite snack: dates and figs. You can dip them in dark chocolate if you want an extra kick. You also have a delicious party snack to offer if you insert an almond in precut dates.

Desserts

This is where your new approach with alternative sugar and different flours will make a difference in your beauty, skin and waistline.

Revise all your favorite recipes and switch to unrefined or gluten free flours. Use xanthan gum for good texture. Sweeten only with stevia, xylitol, coconut sugar, or applesauce (homemade one if possible).

Fruit Crumble with Oats

I am crazy about this recipe! Fill a 9x12 baking dish with slices of any fruit you want (peaches, plums, and red berries) sweetened with 1 tsp. of xylitol. In a bowl, add 1/2 cup of gluten-free flour or spelt flour, 1 cup of oats, 1/2 cup of ground pecan nuts, and 1/2 cup of coconut oil. Add 3 tsp. of xylitol and sprinkle 1 tsp. of cinnamon. Mix well all ingredients. Spread the mixture on top of the fruit. Bake in the oven at 350° for 35 minutes until you see fruit bubbling under the oat crumble. It's irresistible and so healthy!

Fruit Pies

You can't go wrong with fruit pies: it is better to use a thin crust made from unrefined or gluten-free flour (homemade or frozen). Fruit pies are the essence of French baking. Every family has its own recipe; each bakery offers a wide variety of this delicious dessert.

Bake pies with fruit which appeal to you (apples, strawberries, or plums). They should have no creamy filling unless you use dairy-free cream from almond milk or coconut milk (in health food stores). And if you like whipped cream, you can buy healthy whipped cream made from coconut or almond milk (or check on line how to create your own dairy-free whipped cream).

Loaves/Pound cakes

Keep your regular recipe but try to use the right flour, sweeten with stevia or xylitol, and replace butter with grape seed oil. Learn how to adjust the ingredients to bake gluten free pound cakes. You can replace chocolate chips with fruit like raspberries, dried raisins, and little slices of apple. Enjoy your banana bread with walnuts and dark cocoa nibs which are full of antioxidants. Be creative and adapt all your recipes for the best.

Cookies

Cookies are authorized only if you can use the right ingredients: use healthy ones such as dehydrated shredded coconut fat, almond flour, coconut flour, dried fruit, raw cocoa nibs, ground nuts. You are going to be blown away with these "new/old recipes"! Adapt your oatmeal cookies or ginger cookies recipe: you will not be disappointed. And guess what? You family and friends will not see the difference. The only thing they will see is a difference in your looks! You'll have to share your secret because they will not understand how you can allow yourself such desserts without suffering the consequences that typically follow.

You see, this program is not synonymous with restriction but rather restructures your diet with the right ingredients. If you go to restaurants, take your time to select the best meal and keep in mind your beauty food friends. Don't feel guilty if, once in a while, you get off track of your healthy beauty path (but don't overdo it).

This beauty nutrition represents the key to your beauty for many years to come! You're investing in your health and your looks.

Now that you have come so far with these magical ingredients, why don't you try them on your skin? This is the fun part that your face and your body have been waiting for.

Use your beauty foods in your beauty care and makeup!

CHAPTER 2

BEAUTIFYING FOOD IN HOMEMADE BEAUTY PRODUCTS

Now that you've decided to take charge of your beauty strategy from A to Z, discover the magic of the external use of daily foods.

Be logical: if these foods are good internally they can also be beneficial externally. You have in your kitchen the best tools to build your daily beauty routine. These recipes are designed to be simple, fun, and effective. Who doesn't know one old-fashioned beauty recipe? Who hasn't heard of the famous Cleopatra milk bath?

There is nothing new about making DIY (do it yourself) products. Put aside this frenetic desire of buying new beauty products (hoping to get results on your skin). Come back to basics and learn how to customize your beauty care.

Here's why it's worthwhile to create your own products.

Cost

In this world of crisis and financial turmoil, saving money and limiting indulgent sprees is crucial. The ingredients used in the homemade beauty recipes offer a great variety of use; for example, vegetable oil, eggs, honey, all at a very low cost. It's a relief for your wallet!

Omitting Toxicity

According to the latest scientific studies, our beauty creams, shampoos, and makeup are loaded with chemical components. These same studies explain that what you put on your skin will end up in your bloodstream. The Suzuki Foundation explains why some ingredients present in our skin care and cosmetics might be a real health hazard causing things like the disruption of hormones, and cancer. When making your homemade products, you can say goodbye to parabens, petroleum-based products, lead, coal tar colors, sodium lauryl sulfate, 1,4-dioxane, propylene glycol, diazolidinyl, synthetic colors, synthetic polymers and the list goes on. Some of those ingredients are used for your car as brake fluid or antifreeze! Check the label of your beauty products or makeup. You will find other impossible-to-pronounce words. Do you really want this toxic cocktail on your skin and absorbed into your cells?

Effectiveness

Many beauty products contain only two to five percent of active ingredients. Your homemade versions offer one hundred percent active ingredients. Needless to say, you'll see better results. Your personal products improve the skin and hair without irritation or drying side effects. Food-based beauty care has two simultaneous purposes: healing and beautifying.

Pride of DIY (Do It Yourself)

Don't you think it's a personal achievement to be more beautiful every day because you create your own beauty strategy? For me, the admiration and curiosity of people who ask me "which cream do you use to get such glowing skin?" reaffirms my devotion to natural beauty. Play with food and plant based ingredients and fabricate your own elixirs.

Green Attitude

When you make your natural products, you help the planet. There are no packaging or chemical ingredients polluting the earth. Some studies show that toxic ingredients found in cosmetics are ending up in water and affecting fish populations! One more benefit to making your own beauty products is that no animal testing takes place.

Discover a Lost Art

By making your own products, you're reviving the lost art of fabricating creams, lotions, shampoos, and makeup. Follow the wisdom of our ancestors. All the recipes you will find here have been used, tested, and approved for years (back even to Antiquity).

If you're still not convinced, look at the cover of this book. It is a picture of me taken at the age of fifty-one. Thanks to my food-based homemade beauty care and a great nutrition, I could erase pimples, wrinkles, and red patches.

You're going to discover some beauty secrets made with natural ingredients. Some of them are French beauty secrets transmitted from mother to daughter. The day I discovered the little beauty guide of my grandmother, I decided to follow the path of a natural beauty routine. My mother and grandmother both had gorgeous skin and didn't use commercial cosmetic brands or go to a spa.

Speaking about French women beauty, is it a myth or a reality? There is no myth just simple reality. French women aren't born perfect. They follow simple rules and stick with it. They must work to achieve their looks by finding solutions to their beauty concerns with patience and imagination.

I will give you French tips that will help you in your own beauty regimen for the rest of your life.

This is the foundation of a daily French beauty routine:

- Never go to bed without removing any trace of makeup.

- Use homemade facial masks on regular basis (alternate between clarifying, moisturizing, and anti-aging ones).

- Use homemade deep conditioners or treatment to repair your hair and maintain its shine and strength.

- Try to find a simple solution with plants or food-based treatments to fight any esthetic problems.

- Keep a positive attitude concerning your looks, and above all, don't let yourself go and never accept defeat in beauty. If you have cellulite, take action and treat it. If you see wrinkles, embrace them or seek out natural solutions to smooth them. If you have acne, don't cover it with more makeup, create your own products that will help you treat it. These are the reasons why you see mature French women that are still gorgeous when they're fifty years old and older. They do their best to look great even if it's only a simple accessory that can give them allure or style.

French women embody a more natural approach to beauty. They don't rely on esthetic surgery, even if they have the greatest esthetic surgeons in the country. Of course, they know about

Botox and fillers injections, but they consider them a last resort solution.

A French woman wishes *être bien dans sa peau* which could be literally translated as "to be comfortable in her skin". French women accept who they are and don't try to look like somebody else. This includes their assets, but also their flaws. Part of the allure French women have is their attitude and the way they carry themselves. They don't confess how much effort they put into their appearance; they want to look naturally beautiful, but don't strive for perfection.

Now, it's your turn to learn all about French beauty secrets!

Many of the recipes offered in this guide have been used for centuries. In France, women prefer natural skin care. They love to use plants or food-based ingredients because they get results without spending a fortune or compromising their health with synthetic ingredients.

Before beginning this wonderful adventure of natural skin care and the creation of your homemade products, consider this precautionary information:

1. If you have allergies to certain food, there's a good chance that you'll be allergic to them at the epidermal level. If you see any skin reaction or feel irritation, please stop and find an appropriate substitution or an entirely different recipe.

2. Always test products on the inside of your wrist or inner forearm. Wait forty-eight hours to determine your body's reaction.

3. Please keep in mind the varying levels of shelf-life. Some of these homemade products are for one-time use only.

Others can be stored for a few days up to several months in a cool dark area or in the refrigerator.

4. Always select the best products available: organic, natural and/or local food. Buy beauty ingredients from your health food store or online from reputable sites. Check the list available at the end of this book. If you need to use water in the formation of your products, distilled water is a good choice to avoid bacterial contamination.

5. Making your own beauty care products requires the practice of proper hygiene to avoid microbial contamination. Wash your hands. Sterilize your pots and tools by boiling them for at least twenty minutes and dry them well. You should also use tinted glass bottles and close any container tightly after use. Write the date on a label when making your products.

All you'll need to make your own beauty products are basic tools that you can find at your home outfitting store or online. Here's a list to get you started: a food scale, a measuring cup, a tablespoon, a teaspoon, a saucepan, a metal or Pyrex bowl, a blender or food processor, glass or ceramic jars, a dropper, a small hand whisk, colored glass bottles, and an atomizer sprayer.

Which basic ingredients do you need for your beauty care?

- **Food**

- **Vegetable oils**

- **Essential oils**

- **Distilled water**

- **Floral water**

In many recipes, you'll need to use some of the following ingredients:

- **Aloe vera gel**

- **Rosehip oil**

- **Castor oil**

- **Sweet almond oil**

- **Argan oil**

Nature has everything you need to be beautiful! Your beauty products don't have to be complicated to be effective. Rediscover what you have around you.

Choosing the right oil will help you achieve the most from your products. When buying oil, quality matters. Cold pressed oils are preferable.

Here is a list of different vegetable oils and which skin type they suit:

- **Oil for dry skin:** olive oil, argan oil, avocado oil.

- **Oil for mature and sun damaged skin:** rosehip oil, also referred to as Rosa mosqueta oil.

- **Oil for irritated skin:** calendula oil.

- **Oil for normal to combination skin:** apricot kernel oil, wheat germ oil, grape seed oil, sweet almond oil.

- **Oil for acne or oily skin:** hazelnut oil, jojoba oil (keep in the refrigerator if possible).

Essential oils can also be added to your beauty elixirs. Look for the purest quality at your health food stores or online. Essential oils have been used for centuries (Egyptians used them to embalm their mummies). They are distilled or pressed from plants, flowers, and fruit. To use essential oils, you must dilute them in a carrier oil such as grape seed oil, almond oil, or apricot kernel oil. Only tea tree or lavender essential oils can be used directly.

Important Guidelines for Essential Oils Use

- Never apply essential oils directly on the mucous membranes (mouth, eyes).

- Keep out of reach of children.

- Avoid fennel and sage essential oils if you suffer from epilepsy.

- Avoid using essential oils during pregnancy. The following can be used at very low doses: chamomile, jasmine, lavender, ylang-ylang, rose, and rosemary.

- Some essential oils are phototoxic such as bitter orange fruit, grapefruit, lemon fruit, and lime fruit. Avoid applying them on your skin before going out in the sun, otherwise brown spots may occur.

Essential Oils for Your Skin Type

- **Dry skin**: rosewood, ylang-ylang, geranium, neroli

- **Wrinkled and mature skin**: carrot, rose, neroli

- **Oily skin**: eucalyptus, lavender, bay laurel, sage, tea tree

- **Acne skin**: tea tree, lavender, thyme, sage, lemon, rosemary, carrot

BEAUTY FOOD ON YOUR FACE

What does it mean, to be beautiful? The criteria for beauty often come down to an attractive face, particularly your features such as your eyes and nose. A flawless complexion has been and always will be synonymous with real beauty.

The Greek philosopher Aristotle said: *"Personal beauty is a greater recommendation than any letter of reference"*. Looking and feeling good can open doors. So, how do you get a lovely complexion?

You can't change your facial features (unless you undergo plastic surgery), but you can improve your skin quality with a little effort. The most important thing is not to emulate unrealistic beauty icons from magazines. Remember that these pictures have been edited and the models have been photoshopped. Be yourself and find your own beauty!

The recipes in this book will help you look beautiful for years to come.

You should begin with subtle changes, gradually use one homemade product instead of your regular beauty products. Be patient, the results will come.

There is a new beauty movement called slow cosmetic. It has been created by a French man, Julien KAIBECK. He promotes beauty care made with natural ingredients. He is amazing and shows on YouTube how to create, at home, your own cosmetics. So, do the same and begin your wonderful journey in the "beauty food-land!"

Knowing your skin type is crucial to establish the right beauty plan. If necessary, visit a dermatologist to get the information you need.

I thought for years that my skin was only acne-prone; but in fact, it was dry in certain areas. The treatments I used were too severe and caused more breakouts and dehydrated my skin. Thanks to changing my diet and using wonderful natural beauty ingredients, I now have the glowing skin of my dreams!

Each skin type needs specific care or a combination of products. In the next skin care recipes listed in this book, you'll find an abbreviation such as N (normal skin), D (dry skin), M (mature skin), O&A (oily and acne-prone skin), C (combination skin) and AST (all skin types).

Here is a list of skin types:

- **Normal skin:** skin that is well balanced, supple, with no acne (the type of skin that makes your friends jealous).

- **Dry skin:** skin which is delicate with fine texture, invisible pores (lucky!), and prone to wrinkles.

- **Mature skin:** skin that has wrinkles, dark spots, or uneven skin pigmentation, and lacks firmness.

- **Oily and acne-prone skin:** skin which has large pores and can be shiny all over. Oily skin can be acne-prone, usually with inflamed pimples, as well as black and white heads.

- **Combination skin:** skin which is a combination of different skin types; for example, oily in the T-zone and dry on the rest of the face. This type requires a mixture of treatments but can be well controlled by normal skin products too.

Makeup Removers and Cleansers

Don't miss these essential steps to your beauty routine. Makeup removers and cleansers remove dirt and makeup. They prepare your skin to absorb all the benefits of your skin care products.

No excuses! Don't go to bed without cleansing your face. French women don't even think of sleeping with makeup.

Soap is not recommended because it's too harsh. Soap disturbs the delicate balance of your epidermis. Food-based products are the best answer!

Eye Makeup Remover with Oil

Oil melts away makeup very well. I know some French models who only use olive oil to remove their thick eye makeup after a fashion show. Oil can also remove mascara, even waterproof mascara.

Use a cotton ball or a homemade reusable cleansing pad. Dip it in olive oil, argan oil, or sweet almond oil. Swipe gently over your eye area, removing traces of mascara, eye shadow, and eyeliner.

Eye Makeup Remover with Aloe Vera Gel

Proceed the same way as the oil recipe. Aloe vera has great benefits. It helps stimulate eyelashes growth.

Makeup Remover with Oil

Even if you have an oily skin, this recipe will still work for you. Just choose the right oil, for example, apricot kernel oil. This is called the oil cleansing method (OCM). You need to use this method on a regular basis in order to get your skin to adjust. If you have any reaction or don't see good results after two or three weeks, change to another homemade makeup remover.

Apply oil on your skin and massage it well (facial massage=firmer skin) for 1 or 2 minutes. Then, with a wet warm cloth, wipe your face several times, rinsing your cloth with every wipe. You should end up with a clean and supple skin. Some people will not need to apply a moisturizer at this point. It's up to you.

Makeup Remover with Aloe Vera

This one is so refreshing! If you wear heavy foundation or powder, use this first, then finish with a water-soluble cleanser or wash. Remove mascara with oil or pure aloe vera.

Use a small sterilized cream container and put aloe vera gel in it. Add 2 or 3 drops of essential oil (lavender for oily skin, tea tree for acne skin, and rose for normal to dry skin). Mix well. Optional: You can add 1 tsp. of vegetable oil specific to your skin type. Massage into your skin (avoid eyes area). Remove the excess oil with a tissue or washcloth.

Makeup Remover with Honey

Let's get sweet. This recipe was presented in the French beauty workshop, and was the key to my clear and glowing skin.

Wet your skin and apply raw unpasteurized honey on your face (only this type of honey works; it has all the benefits that nature can offer you: anti-bacterial and moisturizing). Massage it. Rinse with warm water and finish with a splash of cold water.

Cleanser with Milk, Heavy Cream, or Cottage Cheese (N/D/C)

Don't laugh! This technique is great and so simple.

You can clean your face with these foods from your refrigerator. Use it like a milky cleanser. This is for one time use only.

Fruit Puree Cleanser (AST except sensitive skin)

French women are addicted to this one.

Choose the fruit you feel is best for you, such as strawberries, ripe papaya, tomato, avocado, green or red grapes. Rub it gently into your skin. Rinse well. If you have any left over, just eat it!

Cleanser with Yogurt and Lemon (O&A)

This recipe leaves your skin smooth and fresh.

Mix 3 tbsp. of yogurt with 3 tbsp. of lemon juice in a bowl. This mixture can be stored in the refrigerator a few days if placed in a tightly sealed container. Massage into your face in a circular motion. You can rinse the cleanser off with warm water or just remove the excess product with a tissue or washcloth.

Soft Cleanser/Makeup Remover (D)

Mix ½ cup of squash juice (use a juicer ahead of time) and 1 ounce of almond oil. Mix well. Apply on your skin with your fingers or with a cotton ball. It can be stored in the refrigerator in a tightly sealed container for a few days.

Milky Rose Cleanser and Makeup Remover (AST)

Mix well 2 tbsp. of heavy cream with 2 tbsp. of raw unpasteurized honey and 1 tbsp. of rose water. Apply on your skin with your fingers or with a cotton ball. It can be stored in a tightly sealed container in the refrigerator for a few days.

Cleanser for Pimples (O&A)

Add 15 drops of lavender essential oil to ½ cup of witch hazel. Store it in a tinted bottle and shake well before use. Apply the cleanser on a cotton ball and wipe your skin. More cleanser recipes for acne are listed in the section *Natural Solutions for Beauty Problems*.

Granulated Cleansers

Semi-scrubby cleansers should be used two or three times a week for a deeper cleanse. They are not true scrubs, as they are made from a milky liquid part (such as plain unsweetened yogurt) and a granulated part.

Yogurt & Salt Cleanser (O&A)

This cleanser will smooth your skin without irritation.

Mix 2 tbsp. of yogurt with 1 tsp. of fine sea salt and massage gently into your skin. Rinse well.

Yogurt & Oats Cleanser (AST)

Mix 2 tbsp. of yogurt with 1 tbsp. of rolled oats or powdered oats. Massage the mixture into your face. Rinse well.

Toners

The use of toner is not necessary, but it's very refreshing. In addition, it helps make sure the skin has no more product residue and can tighten pores. For someone who is in a hurry in the morning, like me, it can be a simple way of removing the oil that accumulates on the skin during the night.

They are so perfect to use before applying any serum or moisturizer. Floral waters are a common ingredient found in homemade toners. You can find them at your local health food store (or learn how to make them yourself).

Choose from the following floral waters:

- Chamomile, rose, and orange water are for dry skin.

- Rosemary, witch hazel, and lavender water are for normal to oily as well as acne-prone skin.

Rose water is a must for French women. It's a tradition to always have a spray bottle of rose water in their bathroom or on the go in their purse.

Did you know? Paul Newman used a bowl filled with ice cubes, splashed the cold water on his face and toned his skin this way before any event. This is a great celebrity beauty secret; firm your skin like a star!

Fruit Peels as Toners (not for sensitive skin)

In the morning, after eating your delicious beauty fruit, use their peel on your skin.

Choose fruits such as peach (D), apple (O&A), lemon and grape (O) or pear (N) and rub its peel on your face gently.

Rose Toner (D)

Mix ½ cup of rose water and 4 tbsp. of distilled water in a bottle (spray bottle is fine too) or just pour rose water in a spray bottle and add 10 drops of rose essential oil. If you want to prepare your own rose water, put a hand full of rose petals in 2.5 Fl. oz. of distilled water. Let sit for 20 minutes and filter. To get a moisturizing toner, use rose water and the same amount of aloe vera distilled water and add 5 drops of chamomile essential oil.

Toner to Minimize Pores (O&A)

I use this recipe on a regular basis.

Mix 1 cup of rose water and 1 ½ cups of witch hazel. Here is another effective recipe: cut 1 cucumber in small cubes and cook it 1 hour in ½ liter of water. Let it cool and filter. Place it in a bottle. It can be kept for up to one week in the refrigerator.

Parsley Toner (O/M)

This toner controls oil and helps firm up the skin.

Put 1 bunch of parsley in 1 liter of water for 24 hours. Pour the parsley water in a bottle. Add 3 drops of tea tree essential oil and 1 tbsp. of apple cider vinegar. It can be kept for 3 or 4 days in the refrigerator.

Italian Parsley Toner (AST)

This is an all-natural anti-wrinkle one for every skin type. My mother has been using it for years and swears by it.

Put 2 bunches of Italian parsley in 1 litre of water and boil it for a few minutes. Let it cool for 30 minutes and pour the parsley water in a bottle. It can be stored one week in the refrigerator.

Green Tea Toner (AST)

This toner stimulates a glow in your complexion. Use loose green tea leaves of great quality, no tea bags. Prepare it like a regular tea.

Put 3 tsp. of green tea in ¼ cup of water. Boil it. Let it cool. Add 3 drops of lavender essential oil and 1 tsp. of aloe vera gel. Mix it well and pour it in a bottle. Store it in the refrigerator.

Facial Steams

Facial steams have been forgotten. You can still see French women using these facial steams to begin with their weekly beauty regimen. They usually do it on the weekend or the day before going out. It might be an old-school technique, but the results are wonderful.

The effectiveness of all your masks, serums, and moisturizers will increase if you take the time to put your head above a bowl filled with steaming water and great ingredients. Don't forget to use a towel and cover your head like a tent.

It relaxes your facial muscles, stimulates your blood circulation, and above all, opens your pores that might be filled with sebum, dirt, and makeup.

Sweat it out! This step should be done after completely removing your makeup or after cleansing.

How often? One or two times per month.

How? Boil mineral water, lower the heat and add herbs (dry or fresh). Steep for 3 minutes. Pour the herbal water into a bowl; add drops of essential oils suited to your skin type. Sit at a table. Drape a towel over your head and your face (to create a tent) and keep your face above the steam for 10 minutes. Listen to some music and relax.

You can create your own treatment combination and choose one of these beauty programs:

- Facial steam + purifying mask

- Facial steam + scrub + moisturizing mask (or firming mask)

Caution: be careful not to burn yourself, and don't use steams if you have active inflamed acne, sensitive skin, or broken facial capillaries.

Flower Steam (AST)

Pour 2 ¾ cups of mineral water over 1 tsp. of chamomile flowers in a bowl. Add 1 tsp. of rose petals. Follow the instructions as described before.

Herbal Steam (C/O&A/M)

Pour 2 ¾ cups of mineral water over 1 tsp. of sage in a bowl. Add 1 tsp. of rosemary. Follow the instructions as described before.

Anti-Aging Steam (D/M)

Pour 2 ¾ cups of mineral water over 1 tsp. of crushed fennel seeds in a bowl. Add 3 drops of rose essential oil. Follow the instructions as described before.

Purifying Steam (O&A)

Pour 2 cups of mineral water over 1 mixed bunch of parsley and thyme in a bowl. Add 2 drops of lemon essential oil. Follow the instructions as described before.

Facial Scrubs

To get radiant and glowing skin, a deep cleanse is required on a regular basis. Once you reach age thirty, the turnover of epidermal cells slows down. All those dead cells need to be buffed away.

Scrubs (and masks) are the best way to renew your skin and stimulate capillary circulation. Only then will your skin be ready for your all-natural beauty products. French women never skip this step, because it adds a glow to their complexion.

How often? Once a week for normal to combination and acne-prone skin. Twice a week for dry skin.

How? Most of the scrubs should be applied in a gentle circular motion. Don't be too aggressive on your skin; it will cause a reaction or irritation. Use a food processor to mix multiple ingredients for your scrubs. If you want to boost the scrubbing effect of a recipe, you can add ½ tsp. of baking soda.

In some beauty books, scrub recipes may call for granulated ingredients such as sugar or salt. I recommend using either those ingredients for your body. Don't be rough with the delicate skin on your face.

Basic Scrub (AST)

This recipe is deep-cleaning but still leaves your skin feeling soft.

Use oat powder (grind rolled oats in your processor) or cornstarch. Put the powder in a glass jar. It will be ready when needed. At the time of use, just take 2 tbsp. of powdered oats or cornstarch, and mix it with 2 tbsp. of plain unsweetened yogurt. Apply to your face and neck. Massage in a circular motion. Rinse well.

Almond Scrub (AST)

Use 2 tbsp. of almond flour or dehydrated coconut fat and mix it with 2 tbsp. of plain unsweetened yogurt. Apply to the face and massage in a circular motion. Rinse well.

Seaweed Scrub (M)

This scrub is full of minerals, making it ideal for mature skin.

Mix 1 tbsp. of dried powdered kelp (or wakame) with 1 tbsp. of milk. Apply to the face and massage in a circular motion. Rinse well.

Raspberry & Powdered Oat Scrub (N/O&A)

The fruit in this recipe enhances the product's scrubbing effect and adds a dose of vitamins to the skin.

Mix 2 tbsp. of mashed raspberries (or 2 strawberries) with 1 tbsp. of powdered oats. Apply to the face and massage in a circular motion. Rinse well.

Peach (or Guava) & Powdered Oat Scrub (D)

Puree 1 peach or guava with 1 tbsp. of powdered oats. Apply on the face and massage in a circular motion. Rinse well.

Dessert Fruity Scrub (AST/not for sensitive skin)

This recipe is so delicious you might decide to eat it!

Puree 2 or 3 strawberries with 1 tbsp. of heavy cream and 1 tbsp. of raw unpasteurized honey. Apply on the face, and massage the scrub in a circular motion. Rinse well.

Facial Masks

You've reached the pinnacle of this beauty food guide. Nature offers so many ingredients to pamper your skin and facial masks are one of the best ways to utilize those ingredients.
Masks have been used for centuries to clean, purify, moisturize, calm, and tone your skin. My grandmother created her own recipes, because there were no commercial options available.

The French beauty workshop instructor explained that these masks are the most beneficial way to improve your skin in less than twenty minutes. It's your turn; find the mask that suits you best (it will be your beauty secret).

Tips:

- Choose organic or local veggies and fruit for your food-based masks. Select great quality products as if you were going to eat your beauty masks. No need to apply pesticides on your face. Fresh fruit stimulate the skin to produce more collagen and help the process of cell renewal. Masks will help deliver antioxidants right to your skin.

- You can do a facial steam before your facial masks or apply a warm cloth to open the pores.

- To keep your mask in place, use gauze or a piece of fabric with three holes for the eyes and mouth over the beauty puree. Lay down and relax.

- If using yogurt in your mask, it should be at room temperature.

- If you use honey, choose only unpasteurized raw honey. Do not heat it. The darker the color, the better.

- Rinse with warm water and then splash with cold water for a firming effect.

- If you feel any irritation, remove the mask and find another one.

- These masks are for one-time use only. Don't keep the leftovers.

Clarifying Masks

How often? Once a week.

Before you discover your beauty food masks, don't forget about clay masks. They are one of the beauty secrets that French women can't live without. A favorite of these women is French green clay.

You can buy the following clays in your local health food store or online:

- **Green or Yellow Clay (C/O):** Green clay comes from bedrock quarries from France. This green clay (as well as yellow clay) is rich in minerals and can extract impurities, including oils and toxic substances.

- **Red Clay (M/N):** This clay is great for normal skin as well as mature skin. It has regenerative properties.

- **French Pink Clay (for sensitive skin)**: This is a mixture of white and red clay, which is calming for irritated skin.

- **White Clay or Kaolin (AST/D)**: It's a very fine clay and is beneficial for all skin types. For dry skin, use it in combination with oil.

- **Rhassoul Clay (AST)**: This clay comes from Morocco. It tones the skin, leaving it smooth.

To prepare a clay mask, you can add mineral water (for oily skin), oil (for dry skin), or honey (for combination skin) to the clay until you get a good thickness. Keep it on for 15 minutes. If your clay mask cracks, you've left it on too long which can dry out your skin.

You can also add 1 tsp. of apple cider vinegar and some essential oils adapted to your skin type to any basic clay mask. For acne-prone skin, add some drops of hazelnut oil. For this type of skin, you will find many more recipes later in the book.

Optional: enjoy a moisturizing mask after a clay mask for a complete beauty treatment.

Papaya Mask (AST/not for sensitive skin)

This is a great mask which contains enzymes that eliminate dead skin cells. Green papaya is even better. This recipe will leave your skin glowing.

Place half of a papaya in a blender and puree it (eat the other half). Apply this puree to your face. Keep it on for 10 minutes, then massage it and rinse it off. You can always add some strawberries for added alpha-hydroxy acid benefits.

Cucumber Mask (O)

A must for oily skin. This mask is refreshing with mild astringent properties.

Mix ¼ of a cucumber with 2 tbsp. of yogurt. Keep it on for 20 minutes and rinse it off. Don't forget the famous cucumber slices on your eyes!

Strawberry Mask (AST/not for sensitive skin)

Do you need to tighten large pores and calm redness? This is your solution.

Mix 2 or 3 strawberries in a blender and apply the puree to your skin. Keep it on for 10 minutes. Massage it and rinse off.

Cherry Mask (D)

Adapted especially for dry skin. Same as above.

Oats & Red Berry Mask (AST)

Get the benefits of the alpha-hydroxy acids of the fruit and scrubby effects of the oats.

Mix 2 tbsp. of powdered oats in a blender with ¼ cup of strawberries, blueberries, and raspberries. I know that's a lot of different berries, but the combination is very effective. Keep it on for 15 minutes. Massage it and rinse off.

White Grape & Almond Mask (O)

Perfect for oily skin.

Puree a hand full of white raisins with 2 tbsp. of almond flour. Keep it on for 10 minutes. Massage it and rinse off.

The Wonderful Egg White Mask (AST)

This is one of my favorite masks; easy and quick to make, plus it firms up the skin. Choose local and organic eggs if possible.

Whisk 1 egg white and apply it with your fingers or a brush. When dry, rinse off. You can also add some lemon drops to the egg white mixture.

Honey & Egg White Mask (O)

A variation to the recipe above. Raw unpasteurized honey has anti-bacterial properties and eggs will help remove black heads.

Mix 1 beaten egg white with 1 tsp. of raw unpasteurized honey. You can also add 6 tbsp. of powdered oats for a scrubbing effect. Keep it on for 10 minutes. Massage in and rinse off.

Moisturizing Masks

How often? 1 or 2 times/week.

These masks are designed to leave your skin supple and soft. You can use moisturizing masks after a purifying mask or after a day out in the harsh elements. French women often use them before leaving their house and going out in public. Your skin will be "addicted" to it (in a good way).

It is your turn to play with your beautifying foods and acquire luminous skin.

The ingredients used for these masks are so delicious that if a drop of food puree goes into your mouth, you know what to do. Eat it! (Imagine if you would do that with commercial masks full of chemicals. Don't even think about it).

Basic Yogurt Mask (AST)

Yogurt contains probiotic agents that nourish and soften the skin. These agents can even lighten skin pigmentation.

Apply 2 tbsp. of plain unsweetened yogurt to your skin. Keep it on for 10 minutes. Rinse well.

Yogurt & Cucumber Mask (N/C)

A variation of the one above.

Mix ½ cucumber (no peel) with 2 tbsp. of yogurt in a blender. Keep it on for 20 minutes then, rinse off.

Honey & Heavy Cream Mask (AST)

Honey is the king beauty food ingredient of facial masks. It makes you skin soft as a baby's. Please, do a test behind your ear before beginning the recipe to check for any reactions.

Mix 2 tbsp. of heavy cream with 1 tbsp. of honey. Optional: you can add any puree of fruit or veggies you like. Keep it on for 15 minutes. Rinse well with warm water.

Yolk & Oil Mask (D)

Ideal for tired and dry skin.

Mix 1 egg yolk with 1 tbsp. of oil of your choice (argan or rosehip oil). Keep it on for 10 minutes and rinse off.

Yolk & Carrot Mask (D/M)

A variation of the previous recipe.

Just add ½ cup of carrot juice to the yolk.

Mayonnaise Mask (AST)

You can use commercial mayonnaise, but a light homemade version will be better for your skin. This mask is very moisturizing.

Mix well 1 yolk with 1 tbsp. of vegetable oil (adapted to your skin type), 1 tbsp. of yogurt, and a few drops of apple cider vinegar. Keep it on for 30 minutes and rinse off.

Avocado Mask (D/M)

This mask is great for nourishing the skin.

Use half of a ripe avocado. Mix it in a blender. Optional: you can add 1 tbsp. of honey and 1 tbsp. of almond flour for extra moisturizing. Keep it on for 20 minutes and rinse off.

Banana Mask (D/M)

You will regain smooth and radiant skin with this mask!

Puree 1 ripe banana and mix it with 1 tbsp. of olive oil and 1 tbsp. of honey. Keep it on for 20 minutes and rinse off.

Peach Mask (AST)

This mask will leave you skin incredibly soft and luminous.

Puree 1 ripe peach and mix it with 1 tbsp. of yogurt and 1 tsp. of honey. Keep it on for 20 minutes and rinse off.

Corn Starch Mask (O)

Perfect for oily skin that might also need to be moisturized.

Mix 2 tbsp. of cornstarch with 1 tbsp. of honey and 1 tbsp. of yogurt or milk. Keep it on for 30 minutes. Rinse off.

Chocolate Mask (AST)

Use chocolate to be beautiful. This recipe calls for raw cocoa powder. Chocolate masks are already trends in spas as they offer moisturizing and repairing benefits.

Mix 2 tbsp. of raw cocoa powder with 2 tsp. of white clay. Add 1/2 tsp. of oil (choose the one that suits best to your skin type) and a little bit of orange juice or mineral water. Apply the mixture with a brush (this mask is a bit messy for finger application). Keep it on for 15 minutes. Rinse off.

Anti-Aging/Rejuvenating Masks

When you think of the word "facelift" in relation to beauty, surgery comes to mind. It can be an extreme approach. If you want to rejuvenate your face, there's an alternative: beauty food! It's all about choosing the right beautifying ingredients.

If you'd like to age gracefully, you'll need to use anti-aging and rejuvenating masks on a regular basis. You'll notice an incredible improvement in your skin's elasticity. It's not a permanent result, but a process you can return to and accumulate the benefits of. Don't forget to apply these masks to your neck and your chest.

French women use many of these anti-aging masks, but they don't advertise it. They develop a weekly ritual that focuses on preventing wrinkles and diminishing signs of aging.

Cultivate a good attitude toward the aging process. Don't try to pretend you are twenty years-old if you are not. Dress accordingly with style adapted to your desire or taste in fashion. Choose one or several of these gorgeous and delicious anti-aging masks to stay beautiful.

Banana & Rose Mask (N/D)

The banana in this mask will soften wrinkles (no Botox).

Puree ½ ripe banana and add 2 drops of rose essential oil. Keep it on for 20 minutes and rinse off.

Creamy Peach Mask (AST)

I love this mask for its ability to erase fine lines.

Puree 2 peaches with 2 tbsp. of heavy cream. Keep it on for 20 minutes and rinse off.

Supreme Fruity Mask (N/D)

It has all the benefits of fruit and cream. This mask will give you a glowing complexion. It will refresh and revitalize tired-looking skin.

Mix in a blender ½ banana with 2 strawberries. Add 2 tsp. of honey and 2 tbsp. of heavy cream. Apply on your face and keep it on for 20 minutes. Rinse off.

Cabbage Mask (AST)

Not the typical mask, but so effective for relaxing wrinkles.

Juice ½ of a green cabbage and combine with 1 tsp. of honey. Keep it on for 30 minutes and rinse off.

Milk Chocolate Mask (AST)

Soften fine lines and wrinkles with this recipe. Use the same raw cocoa powder as listed in the previous chocolate recipe.

Mix the same amount of chocolate to the equal amount of milk. Use almond or coconut milk if you prefer. Keep it on for 20 minutes and rinse off.

Did you know? You can also do an eye mask to refresh and brighten the skin around your eyes. Here are 2 wonderful masks. They are safe for the delicate area around the eyes. I learned about these 2 eye masks while attending a beauty workshop:

- Apply 1 whipped egg white mixed with 1 tsp. of honey. Keep on for 5 minutes and rinse off.

- Remove the white membrane inside the eggshell and apply it under your eyes. Keep on for 5 minutes, and then wipe off.

Rejuvenating Almond Mask (N/D)

A perfect mask to get a radiant complexion and to erase fine lines.

Mix 2 ½ tbsp. of almond flour with 2 tbsp. of witch hazel. Keep on for 25 minutes and rinse off.

Rejuvenating Pineapple Mask (D/tired Skin)

It will revive any dull skin.

Puree 2 pineapple slices with 3 tsp. of olive oil. Keep on for 15 minutes and rinse off.

Rejuvenating Carrot Mask (N/D)

Carrot is a life-saver from Mother Nature. My mother is still using it and she looks amazing.

Puree 1 ripe avocado with 1 cooked carrot, ½ cup heavy cream and 2 tbsp. of honey. Optional: add 1 egg yolk. Keep it on for 20 minutes and rinse off.

Rejuvenating Berry Mask (AST)

This mask stimulates the production of collagen. Choose the vegetable oil suited to your skin type.

Puree 1/4 cup of red berries and 1/4 cup of red grapes with 1/2 tbsp. of vegetable oil. Grape seed oil works well in this recipe. Keep on for 20 minutes and rinse off.

Firming Masks

These masks offer all the benefits of the previous ones but add a slight firming and tightening effect that is great for skin lacking elasticity.

Egg White Magic Mask (N/O/A)

The best quick fix you can find. Do it several times a week.

Just use 1 beaten egg white and apply to your skin with a brush or finger. Keep on until dry and rinse off.

Apple Juice Mask (AST)

Get an instant "lift job".

Mix 1 cup of yogurt with 4 tbsp. of fresh apple juice and 1 egg white. Keep it on for 10 minutes and rinse off.

Grape Mask (D/M)

Grape is a major ingredient of many anti-aging skin care brands in France.

Puree 5 or 6 grapes with 1 tbsp. of heavy cream. Keep it on for 20 minutes and rinse off.

Honey Mask (AST)

Use it before going out, a photo shoot or any time you want to look good. This is one of the secrets French models and actresses use to look their best.

Mix 1 tbsp. of honey with 1 egg white. Keep it on for 10 minutes. Rinse off with warm water, finishing with a splash of cold water.

Strawberry Mask (AST/not for sensitive skin)

Easy and delicious!

Apply a puree of 4 strawberries. Keep on for 10 minutes and rinse off.

Seaweed Mask (D)

Very revitalizing, thanks to the minerals.

Mix 1 tbsp. of powdered seaweed (wakame or kelp) with rose water and make a paste. Add ½ tbsp. of olive oil. Optional: 2 drops of rose essential oil. Keep it on for 20 minutes and rinse off.

Seaweed Mask (N/O)

Mix 1 tbsp. of powdered seaweed with 1 tsp. of aloe vera gel and 2 drops of ylang-ylang essential oil. Keep on for 20 minutes and rinse off.

Oats & Honey Mask (C)

Mix 2 tbsp. of powdered oats with 2 tsp. of honey. Keep on for 20 minutes and rinse off with warm water.

Glowing Skin Masks

If you want to illuminate your complexion before an event or enjoy radiant skin any time, choose one of these masks and glow! Your skin will become healthier and more luminous by the day.

Basic Glowing Skin Mask (AST)

Mix 1 egg yolk with fresh orange juice and add 1 or 2 tbsp. of yogurt. Keep on for 20 minutes and rinse off.

Carrot Mask (AST)

This is a liquid mask that is very effective.

Juice 1 carrot and 1 orange and mix in 1 tbsp. of honey. Keep on for 20 minutes and rinse off.

Creamy Carrot Mask (D/M)

Puree 1 cooked carrot with 1 ripe avocado. Add 2 tbsp. of heavy cream. Mix well. Keep on for 20 minutes and rinse off.

Simple Fruit Puree Mask (AST/not for sensitive skin)

You will get the benefits of alpha hydroxy acids or AHAs, which are found in food enzymes. They eliminate fines lines, remove dead skin cells, and brighten dull skin. Gorgeous and radiant complexion guaranteed!

Puree one fruit of your choice such as mangoes, grapes, cherries, papayas. Optional: add yogurt for thicker consistency. Keep on for 15 minutes and rinse off.

Moisturizers/Serums/Lotions

Commercial companies are always looking for new ways to market their products. When it comes to moisturizers, this is often in the form of a "miracle" ingredient. Don't be fooled, look at the label of these products and try to understand their composition. It's not easy, right? Why would you want to apply parabens, preservatives, and synthetic silicones on your skin (and pay for it)?

Let's come back to natural and low-cost moisturizers. Put on your face what you can eat (or almost)! You don't need to be a biochemist to create your own beauty elixirs.

Here are some guidelines to create your own products:

1. Maintain a rigorous hygiene when preparing your beauty care. Sterilize your tools (spoon, small whisk, pots, glass, bottle, except plastic one of course) in boiling water for at least 20 minutes and dry them well.

2. Keep your products in the refrigerator for future use. If you want, you can use a natural preservative such as grapefruit seed extract (GSE).

3. Use a tinted glass jar or bottle if possible.

4. Use only high-quality ingredients.

5. Occasionally, you might need to shake or whip any mixture with oil to avoid separation of the ingredients.

6. Check for any allergy to essential oils, aloe vera, or natural preservatives.

7. Prepare only small batches to avoid spoiling. You can use grapefruit seed extract as an anti-microbial agent. Besides grapefruit seed extract, you can use bee propolis

as a preservative. It's used in more elaborate beauty recipes and is very effective.

8. If you want to add a nice scent to your creams, add a few drops of vanilla extract, fruit extract and/or geranium essential oil.

How to apply your moisturizer? The best way is to apply with a tapping movement; this stimulates micro-capillary circulation. For the eyes, do the same from the internal corner of the eye to the external corner.

When to apply moisturizer? You need to moisturize your skin every morning with a targeted product (anti-shine, firming, UV protection) adapted to your skin type. At night, apply a serum or a specific product (anti-wrinkle, antioxidant) when your skin cells are in the renewal process. Even oily skin might need a touch of moisturizer.

Did you know? You need to change or alternate products as your skin gets used to them. Also, adapt your products according to the season: lighter in summer, richer in winter.

Floral Water (hydrolat or herbal distillate)

In France, you always find a floral water bottle on a bathroom counter. French women can't live without it. They use floral water after sport activities, after applying makeup to set it, and to refresh their looks on the go. Hydrolats are the by-products of plant steam distillation when obtaining essential oils. Floral sprays are a great solution for oily and acne-prone skin because they moisturize without adding more oil to the skin.

Use the floral water that corresponds with your skin type: rose water (D), orange flower water (N/C), lavender or witch hazel water (O&A). You can add to your hydrolat a few drops of essential oils of your choice.

They offer refreshing, balancing, healing, and moisturizing benefits. Just spray it on your face and go! You can buy them in reputable health food stores or online. You can use floral water in the same way as a toner just before applying your serum. Leaving your skin slightly damp will ensure your skin absorbs the product.

Here is a simple recipe to make your own rose water:

Place 1 cup of rose petals (choose pesticide-free ones to ensure your rose water is high quality) and 2 cups of distilled water in a glass or ceramic bowl. Pour boiling water into the bowl and cover with a lid. Let it sit until water cools down, then strain. Pour into a glass jar and close the lid tightly. This can be kept up to one month in the refrigerator.

Vegetable Oils

Consider moisturizing with simple vegetable oils. They can be used by themselves or combined with aloe vera gel to moisturize the skin naturally. I know many gorgeous women who swear by them and will not use anything else. My mother and grandmother proved to me that simple vegetable oil could protect and preserve the skin until an advanced age. They had almost no wrinkles or brown spots. They were my inspiration to true natural beauty.

Refer to the *Beautifying Food in Homemade Beauty Products* section found in Chapter 2 to determine the oil best suited to your skin type.

Below are other beautifying oils which you might consider using alone or in combination with other ingredients:

- **Argan Oil (D/M)** is a rare oil from the Argan tree found in Morocco. Dry mature skin loves it as it makes skin smooth and radiant, if used as a regular moisturizer.

- **Sweet Almond Oil (AST)** is rich in vitamins A, B, and E. This oil nourishes the skin and helps to prevent signs of aging. It is wonderful as an eye makeup remover and helps eliminate dark circles.

- **Rosehip Oil (D/M)** is a wonder; very rich in vitamin C and not greasy. This is *the* anti-wrinkle oil that you should use in your daily routine.

- **Wheat Germ Oil (N/D)** is firming and is best used with a carrier oil such as grape seed oil or sweet almond oil.

- **Evening Primrose Oil (M)** is a rich source of essential fatty acids (gamma linoleic acid or GLA). This oil softens skin and restructures collagen fibers for anti-aging benefits. It is recommended for eczema and psoriasis. It can be used with a carrier oil such as grape seed oil or sweet almond oil.

- **Borage Seed Oil (D/M)** contains the highest amount of gamma linoleic acid (GLA). It is recommended for eczema, psoriasis, and prematurely aging skin. Caution: don't use this oil if you suffer from hepatic disorders or during pregnancy.

- **Castor Oil (AST)** is just amazing. Derived from the castor plant, this oil is very moisturizing and best used at night. It also plumps the skin and smoothes lines.

- **Macadamia Oil (D/M)** helps preventing and delaying skin aging by its high content in palmitoleic acid. It will also calm dry itchy skin.

- **Coconut Oil (N/D/M)** is very moisturizing and blocks 20 percent of UV rays. It is slightly comedogenic. Use only cold-pressed coconut oil.

For more benefits, add essential oils adapted to your skin (a few drops should be enough). Don't forget to put your oily elixir in a tinted bottle.

Here are some recipes combining lots of ingredients described earlier. They are very simple moisturizing options. You will get amazing result with basic homemade beauty recipes.

Basic Serum (AST)

This serum can be used also as a moisturizer for oily skin. In general, serums are great to apply to your skin at night (by themselves or followed by other products). Don't forget to change with the seasons: more aloe vera in summer and less in winter.

Mix 2 parts aloe vera gel with 1 part vegetable oil adapted to your skin type. Whip the mixture with a whisk for 2 minutes. I recommend buying a small whisk just for your beauty needs. Optional: add essential oils adapted to your skin type. Keep the mixture stored in the refrigerator. You can add a few drops of grapefruit seed extract as a natural preservative.

Anti-Wrinkle Serum (D/M)

This is a great serum which I first learned about at a beauty workshop. The beauty instructor, sixty years of age, used it all her life and she looked very young!

Same recipe as above but you can choose rosehip oil for anti-aging benefits or use 1 part aloe vera gel and 1 part rosehip oil.

Basic Moisturizing Lotion (AST)

Lotions are lighter than a cream and might better suit your needs in summer. Use ingredients that are adapted to your skin type.

In a tinted bottle or old sterilized jar, pour equal parts vegetable oil and floral water or distilled water. Shake well or whisk well before use to avoid separation. You can add some drops of grapefruit seed extract as natural preservative.

Island Beauty Oil (N/D/M)

It's a dream to use this oil all year around. Everybody should have extra virgin coconut oil for cooking and beautifying!

Mix 2 tbsp. of coconut oil with 4 to 5 drops of an essential oil suited for normal to dry skin (ylang-ylang, neroli, and geranium). Keep the mixture in the refrigerator.

Basic Aloe Vera Cream (AST)

A heavier version of the basic serum. I love this one as it gives such a glow to my skin!

Mix 1 part aloe vera gel with 1 part vegetable oil adapted to your skin type. Use a small whisk to mix it well. Store the cream in the refrigerator.

Basic Day/Night Cream (AST)

This recipe is the only one which calls for beeswax. Beeswax is a great thickening and emulsifying agent. You can adapt this recipe to your skin type with the right choice of oil and essential oils.

Mix ½ cup of oil (almond oil or grape seed oil) with 2 tbsp. of beeswax in a bowl. Place the bowl in a double boiler. When the beeswax is melted, remove the bowl and add ½ cup of rose water and 3 or 5 drops of essential oils adapted to your skin type. Mix thoroughly. Put the mixture immediately in a sterilized container, stirring to avoid separation. Close tightly when the mixture is cool.

Hazelnut Cream (O&A)

This cream needs to be kept out of light for 2 days after preparation for all the ingredients to settle.

Mix ½ cup of hazelnut oil with 2 drops of tea tree essential oil and 2 drops of lavender essential oil.

Night Cream (O)

It's a variation of the hazelnut cream. The higher concentration of essential oil will help fight breakouts while sleeping. Apricot kernel oil also works well in this recipe.

Mix ½ cup of oil with 5 drops of tea tree essential oil and 5 drops of lavender essential oil.

Anti-Aging Night/Day Elixir (N/D/M)

A wonderful oil treatment which firms and revitalizes mature skin.

Mix well 1/2 cup of rosehip oil with 10 drops of carrot essential oil. Store in a tinted bottle.

Tip: the best anti-aging essential oils for all skin type are: geranium, myrrh and frankincense. Add 5 drops (or a mixture of them) of the essential oils of your choice into 2 tbsp. of "your" carrier oil.

For the beauty of your eyes:

Basic Eye Gel (AST)

Mix well 1 tsp. of aloe vera gel with 9 drops of jojoba oil and put in a small sterilized eye cream container with a tightly sealed lid. Keep in the refrigerator.

Moisturizing Eye Cream (N/D)

This recipe is very hydrating and has anti-wrinkle benefits for the delicate eye area.

Mix 1 oz. of jojoba oil with 1 tbsp. of rosehip oil and ½ tsp. of castor oil. Keep in the refrigerator.

Fresh Cucumber Eye Gel (N/O/C)

This gel is so refreshing!

Juice ¼ of a cucumber and whisk in 1 oz. of aloe vera gel. You can keep it in the refrigerator for two days.

Did you know? Castor oil is wonderful for crow's feet. Getting results is easy, just apply it at night.

BEAUTY FOOD ON YOUR BODY

Your body can benefit from the amazing ingredients found in your kitchen and in nature. Your neck and chest area can be treated with facial products after you turn forty, particularly if you've spent a lot of time in the sun. With age, you might consider body lotions and skin care products that contain anti-aging properties too. Discover wonderful recipes that your body has been waiting for.

Body Scrubs

Without scrubs, skin doesn't glow. It's necessary to remove the dead cells that accumulate on your epidermis. Your body lotion will be absorbed more, offering you better results. French women have a great interest in scrubs to get their body skin glowing. They love to show off their skin, especially in summer while wearing a summer dress. If you incorporate body scrubs into your beauty routine, you'll be proud to show off your beautiful skin too.

Beauty tools you should have: a soft vegetable fiber brush (found in your local health food store), or a loofah, or scrubby gloves, or all of them!

Some beauty specialists recommend doing dry skin brushing with a soft vegetal brush on daily basis. This will help fight cellulite.

Try to do a body scrub every week. Be careful; don't overdo it especially if you are using rougher exfoliating ingredients. If you have sensitive skin, acne-prone skin, or varicose veins you should not use scrubs. Nature offers you many options from very mild to grainy scrubs.

How? Before any exfoliation, humidify your skin in the shower first. Then, use circular soft massage strokes when applying a scrub and rinse.

All these scrubs recipes are for one time use only.

Basic Body Sugar Scrub

Sugar is a wonderful exfoliator. You can also substitute salt for sugar or use it in combination with sugar.

Mix 1 cup of brown sugar with olive oil to get a smooth paste. You can select the oil of your choice for this recipe (for example, coconut oil). Put it in a clean plastic container. Humidify your skin and apply the scrub in a circular motion. Rinse well.

Island Scrub

The exotic fragrance of this scrub is addictive, and it leaves the skin so smooth.

Mix in a blender 3 tbsp. of dry shredded coconut, ½ cup of plain yogurt and 2 ½ tbsp. of honey. Optional: add a few drops of vanilla extract.

Almond Scrub

This is a French favorite.

Mix 3 tbsp. of almond flour with 2 tbsp. of honey. Don't worry, you won't be sticky using this recipe.

Salt Scrub

This scrub is not recommended for sensitive skin.

Mix 4 tbsp. of jojoba oil or argan oil with 5 tbsp. of coarse salt.

Lulur Treatment

This treatment is used in Indonesia to prepare brides for their wedding night. This version will make your skin incredibly smooth and will leave a sensual scent.

Mix well 2 1/2 cups of rice powder, 2 tsp. of ground turmeric, and ½ tsp. ginger powder. Set aside. Apply the oil of your choice on your body. I like adding a few drops of jasmine essential oil to this step. Then, humidify your skin in the shower or bath. Apply the scrub powder over oiled skin in a circular motion. Then, give yourself a massage with plain yogurt. Rinse thoroughly. After, you can enjoy an aromatic bath with herbs of your choice (rose petals, basilica).

Body Cleansers (Shower and Bath)

You won't believe how easy it is to create your own body cleanser. Forget all those harsh chemicals found in commercial body cleansers. Your skin needs to be washed with natural ingredients to find its own balance and beauty. Use liquid castile soap and essential oils.

You can prepare in advance a bottle of your body cleanser. By adding a few drops of grapefruit seed extract, your cleanser will keep for a month.

Morning Shower Gel

Fresh and effective to wake you up the natural way!

Mix well 1 cup of castile soap (you can buy it at your local health food store) with 1 tbsp. of jojoba oil. Add 5 drops of peppermint essential oil and 2 drops of rosemary essential oil.

Relaxing Shower Gel

An anti-stress concoction.

Mix well 1 cup of castile soap with 1 tbsp. of coconut oil. Add 5 drops of lavender essential oil.

Anti-Odor Shower Gel

Mix well 1 cup of castile soap with 1 tbsp. of witch hazel. Add 3 drops of tea tree essential oil and 2 drops of rose essential oil.

Moisturizing Shower Gel

Mix well 1 cup of castile soap with 3 tbsp. of almond or coconut milk.

If you prefer to take a bath, the recipes below are for you. You'll have a choice between a relaxing recipe, a romantic one or a therapeutic one. Before all, relax your body and mind.

Take a bath and enjoy a perfect spa experience at home (soft music and candles); this is your time in your beauty sanctuary!

Depending on what you prefer, create your own signature bath. You might decide to have an herb infused bath. French women like to use herbal baths for therapeutic and beauty purposes.

For this type of bath, use a knee-high nylon sock; cut it at half way and put in the herbs or flowers you want to use. Place it under the water flow. You can attach it to keep it in place. A little gauze sachet is nice too. Alternatively, prepare a nice amount of tea and pour it in your bath.

Sleeping Bath

Very calming. While soaking, drink a cup of herbal tea.

Put 1 cup of chamomile flower into a gauze sachet (or one knee-high nylon sock) and place it under the water flow.

Epsom Salt Bath

The best bath to relax muscle after exercise.

Add 2 1/2 cups of Epsom salts to your bath water.

Energy Bath

This bath will boost your circulation and help you to re-energize.

Mix 1 tbsp. of sweet almond oil in a bottle with 3 drops of lavender essential oil and 2 drops of grapefruit essential oil. Shake well and add it to your bath water.

Dead Sea Salt Bath

Very detoxifying and full of minerals! You can find these salts in your local health food store.

Put 1 cup of Dead Sea salts in your bath water.

Himalayan Salt Bath

Another recipe full of minerals.

Put 1 cup of this salt in your bath water. Check at your local health food store and get a coarse version of this salt.

Oats Bath

This bath is so moisturizing! Put the powdered oats in a gauze sachet to avoid any plumbing problems.

Place 1 cup of powdered oats in a little sachet (or one knee-high nylon sock) and let it float in your bath water.

Seaweed Bath

Ideal for cellulite problems and weight loss. This is a technique used in many spas all over Europe. In Brittany, a gorgeous area of France, you will find spa centers that only offer seaweed baths, seaweed treatments, seaweed body wraps, and seaweed meals.

Add to your bath 1 cup or more of your favorite seaweed. Any edible one can be used.

Citrus Bath

Very refreshing. This recipe feels like you're been bathed in lemonade. Just don't sunbathe afterwards, doing so could cause a phototoxic reaction and promote brown spots.

Add fresh slices of lemon and/or orange to your bath.

Anti-Aging Bath

Great for dry and mature skin.

Mix 3 tbsp. of wheat germ oil in a bowl with carrier oil such as grape seed oil. Add 2 or 3 cups of whole milk to the oily mixture. Mix well. Add it to your bath water.

Cleopatra Bath

The best and most famous bath from Egyptian times! Cleopatra knew the smoothing benefits of milk. One problem: it is not cheap or easy to find donkey milk. Your best substitute is powdered goat's milk from your health food store. If you want, you can also use nut or seed milk, coconut, or almond milk. This recipe is one of my favorites.

Warm 1 or 2 cups of milk in a pan of your choice and mix it with 1 tbsp. of honey. Remove from the heat. Then add 10 drops of ylang-ylang or rose essential oil, and pour it into your bath. Another version is to dilute 1 cup of powdered milk with water in a bowl and pour it in the bath. You can also add 3 tbsp. of heavy cream to the water.

Body Lotions

Gorgeous and radiant skin is rooted in proper moisturization. The same attention you devote to your face needs to be practiced on other areas of your body that are vulnerable to aging, such as neck and feet.

Dry vegetable oils are the perfect ingredient to use in your body lotion arsenal. They don't leave an oily feeling on your skin and are quickly absorbed. Your skin will be soft and supple.

Here are some options:

- **Jojoba Oil** has a dry texture. This oil has anti-aging and protective properties. It's ideal for any skin type. For dry skin, you can mix it with other oils for more moisturizing effects.

- **Hazelnut Oil** also has a dry texture. This oil offers calming properties. It is known for softening stretch marks and scars. Ideal for any type of skin (oily skin loves it).

Tip: when applying oils to your skin, wait for them to be absorbed before dressing. This will ensure you don't stain your clothes.

Body Oil

I love this recipe. The beauty workshop instructor told me it was the simplest and most effective way to moisturize the body.

Mix 1 part olive oil with 2 parts hazelnut oil. To add a scent, use essential oils that speak to you. Be careful with the essential oils, some of them are phototoxic.

Honey Body Lotion

Don't worry; you won't be sticky.

Mix well 1 tbsp. of honey, 1 cup of apricot kernel oil (or hazelnut oil) and 1/2 cup of heavy cream. Pour it in a bottle. Keep it in the refrigerator.

Aloe Vera Gel & Rosehip Oil Body Lotion

Depending of the moisturizing level you need, add more rosehip oil. This body lotion is very effective for sun-damaged skin or as a prevention treatment.

Whisk together 1 tbsp. of aloe vera gel and 15 to 18 drops of rosehip oil. Whisk well, until it looks like a cream and pour into an old sterilized cream jar. You can prepare 2 or 3 times the amount for a bigger batch.

Aloe Vera & Vegetable Oil Body Lotion

This recipe can be done the same way as the previous one.

Use the vegetable oil that is the best suited for your skin. Whisk well.

Special Neck Care

Many times, I saw my mom and aunts use the combination of a mask followed by an anti-aging lotion. They knew that the first signs of aging appear on the neck.

Make a puree of tomatoes and apply it to your neck. Relax for 20 to 45 minutes. Rinse off. Then apply the rosehip body lotion on your neck with upward strokes.

Special Elbow Care

Exfoliate your elbows with a mixture of almond flour and a few drops of lemon juice. You can also substitute baking soda for almond flour. Afterwards, massage with your preferred oil elixir.

Special Foot Care

Sweet almond oil is wonderful when incorporated into a foot massage, particularly on dry and cracked heels. You can also use half of an avocado peel. Every time you eat one, think of your feet in need! Here is another solution for dry and cracked heels: puree half of an avocado and apply it to your feet. Wear old socks and go to bed with it! In summer, if you want a refreshing and cooling gel, use aloe vera gel with a few drops of mint essential oil.

Shaving Gel

Aloe vera gel is a simple and refreshing shaving lotion. You can add some olive oil, which will create a moisturizing effect.

Mix well 1 part olive oil with 3 parts aloe vera gel. Store in a plastic container.

After-Shave Lotion

The best anti-irritation and smoothing after-shave, even for men!

Mix 2 tsp. of aloe vera gel with 1 tsp. of jojoba oil. Add 8 drops of lavender essential oil for the anti-bacterial benefits.

Sugar Waxing

Rediscover the purity and effectiveness of waxing; your legs will be soft for weeks! It has been used for centuries and offers a professional result without the mess of the wax.

Use raw or regular sugar. Mix well 1 cup of sugar with 2 tbsp. of water and 2 tbsp. of lemon. Bring to boil in a small pan on medium heat for 5 to 7 minutes, stirring constantly. When all the sugar is dissolved, and the mixture is at body temperature, immediately apply it on your leg with a spatula. Then place cotton strips over the sugar mixture and firmly press several times. Quickly pull off the cotton piece against the direction of your hair growth. Rinse well with cold water.

BEAUTY FOOD ON YOUR HAIR AND NAILS

Our hair and nails tell us a lot about the state of our health. They represent the best reflection of any imbalance that could occur in your metabolism. Sickness, vitamin deficiencies, and stress signs show through our hair and nails. External aggressions like wind, sun exposure, overuse of a flat iron or blow dryer, chlorinated water, and home household products (for the nails) can be very damaging.

The use of commercial chemical cocktails in your hair care products, nail polish, and nail polish remover could be the explanation for your bad hair day and brittle nails.

Why not come back to these beautifying foods offered by Mother Nature? You'll be surprised how your hair and nails will regain their strength and beauty in a limited time!

You already have the foundation to transform yourself with the nutrition indicated in the beginning of this beauty guide. Now, learn how to get healthy and shiny hair with simple solutions!

First, you need to know your hair type:

- **Dry Hair:** brittle, dull, prone to breakage and splits ends.

- **Oily Hair:** greasy, has a shiny or oily look with no volume.

- **Normal Hair:** bouncy, shiny, elastic, full of body (as seen in commercials).

- When tailoring your hair care, also keep its thickness and frizz level in mind.

Tips:

- Try to avoid any heat damage with hair styling tools. I have great hair because I limit the use of hair styling tools. I take my time and dry my hair naturally or put some big rollers in and enjoy my afternoon at home.

- Try not to wash your hair every day. You will see the difference!

- Buy a great quality brush with natural bristles.

- Use only natural products or DIY products made with beauty food ingredients!

Hair Masks

Hair masks are the secret to gorgeous hair. There are many foods that have wonderful benefits for your hair. French women have one day per month set aside for this process. They hate to be seen with a hair mask on, but they will be proud to show off their shiny hair the day after!

Hair masks or deep hair treatments should be done 1 or 2 times per month. Too many deep treatments can disturb the natural balance of your hair. These hair mask recipes target specific concerns and should be used immediately.

For very dry hair, it is better to do a mask before the shampoo and leave it for 30 minutes or longer (if your hair is damaged and needs a deeper treatment). For normal hair, apply the mask after the shampoo for 10 to 15 minutes and rinse well.

Grape Seed Oil & Egg Hair Mask (normal to dry/fine hair)

I forgot about this mask for the longest time. When I adopted a more natural beauty routine, I referred to this recipe and it gave my hair incredible shine and strength. Thanks to this recipe, I still have gorgeous medium length hair at fifty-one years old.

Pour the right proportion of oil necessary for the length of your hair into a glass or stainless-steel bowl (approximately ¼ cup for short hair, ½ cup for medium, and ¾ cup for long). Place the bowl in a larger pan or bowl filled with hot water. When the oil is warm, thoroughly mix in 1 egg yolk. Apply on wet hair, cover with a plastic shower cap or plastic wrap. Then, wrap a warm towel around your head. The heat opens the hair shaft and allows the mixture to penetrate deeply.

Olive or Coconut Oil Hair Mask (normal to dry/coarse hair)

Use the same preparation as above, but with olive or coconut oil. It will leave a delicate tropical scent on your hair.

Infused Oil Hair Mask (oily hair)

Even oily hair can benefit from a mask.

Infuse fresh rosemary and sage leaves (or thyme instead of sage) into 1 cup of grape seed oil for 2 weeks. Use a sterilized glass jar with a tight-fitting lid; store away from sunlight and turn the jar upside down at least twice a day. Use it the same way as the two previous masks.

Banana Hair Mask (dull/tired hair)

This mask could also be used as a conditioner.

Puree 1 ripe banana with 1 cup of warm water. For coarse hair, add 1 tbsp. of coconut oil. For fine hair, add 1 tbsp. of grape seed oil. Apply on your hair. Keep it on for 15 minutes. Rinse well and proceed to shampoo.

Avocado Hair Mask (dry hair)

This recipe can also double as a conditioner. French women with dry hair can't live without it!

Puree 1 ripe avocado with 1 egg yolk. Apply on your hair. Keep it on for 15 minutes. Rinse well and proceed to shampoo.

Seaweed Hair Mask

Full of minerals, this mask stimulates hair growth. It also acts as a cleanser to remove dirt and hair product residue.

Soak a hand full of seaweed of your choice for 20 minutes. Puree and apply on your hair. Leave it on for 20 minutes. Rinse well. Proceed to shampoo.

Shampoos

With so many choices at the drugstore, it may seem like an inconvenience to make your own. Believe me, it's worth it! Here is why...

According to multiple international studies, the composition of commercial shampoos might harm your hair *and* your body. Many common ingredients have ominous names like sodium lauryl sulfate (or sodium laureth sulfate), polyethylene glycol and let's not forget parabens. Commercial shampoos contain harsh detergents that strip your hair of its natural oil and leave it dull, lifeless, and dry.

The worst is yet to come! According to reports made by various toxicology agencies, the regular use of these synthetic chemicals could expose your body to potential risk of cancer and hormone imbalance. Toxins are absorbed through the skin. So, what can you do?

When in doubt, return to a simple and safe solution.

Basic Shampoo

Buy liquid Castile soap. In a plastic bottle, pour 2 parts Castile soap with 1 part distilled water. Add your favorite essential oil and shake well. A nice conditioner and a rinse with vinegar should follow this shampoo, as Castile soap might leave a residue. The addition of aloe vera or eggs is also beneficial in this recipe.

Egg Shampoo

This is an old-fashioned shampoo that my grandmother used all her life. This recipe is great for dry hair.

Beat 2 eggs and give yourself a nice scalp massage as you work the mixture through your hair. Rinse with warm water. Proceed with a rinse suited to your hair color (which we'll talk about later in this section).

Cabbage Shampoo

If the cabbage scent is not appealing to you, add an essential oil of your choice. This is a very effective shampoo or treatment for oily hair.

Add to the basic shampoo 2 tbsp. of cabbage juice (add less than this is you have short hair) and ½ tsp. of aloe vera gel. Shake well, and then apply. Leave on for 3 minutes. Rinse.

Dry Shampoo

In a hurry? This recipe is your go-to.

Take 1 tbsp. of rolled oats and rub gently through your hair all the way to your ends. Shake your head well. Comb with a wide-tooth comb.

Conditioners

Labels that promote a fruity or exotic scent for conditioners are also guilty of using harsh chemical ingredients. In fact, the actual proportion of natural ingredients in commercially made hair products is around three percent. Food-based DIY products will help you get gorgeous, manageable, and shiny hair with one hundred percent active ingredients.

Always rinse well after conditioner use, once with warm water, a second time with cold water to get an extra shine and to close the hair follicles.

Beer Conditioner

Natural beauty can be fun, and this recipe is a proof. Take a swig of beer for yourself! It will give an incredible shine and will boost the volume of your hair.

Warm 1 cup of beer. Apply thoroughly to hair and scalp. Rinse well.

Island Conditioner

Here is a real tropical conditioner. Your hair will smell so nice and will be shiny. This is great for dry/coarse hair. For dry fine/hair, use less coconut oil or replace it with coconut milk.

Mix ½ cup of mayonnaise (your own mayonnaise is ideal, but a good organic one will work too) with 1 tbsp. of coconut oil. Mix well. Apply throughout your hair. Leave on for 5 to 10 minutes. Rinse well.

Fruity Conditioner

The result of this conditioner is amazing. It will leave your hair silky, shiny, and moisturized to perfection!

Mix 1 cup of plain yogurt, milk or nut milk with a fruit puree of your choice: 1 ripe banana (for frizzy and dry hair), or 1 ripe papaya (for oily hair), or a few strawberries (for normal hair). Apply to your hair. Keep the conditioner on for 30 minutes. Rinse well.

Mayonnaise Conditioner

Easy and effective for all hair types: it gives to your hair a lovely shine and great body.

The smell of mayonnaise doesn't linger, but you can add your favorite essential oil for a mild scent. Apply it throughout your hair. For a deeper treatment, cover your hair with a shower cap. Keep it on for 15 minutes. Rinse well.

Plain Yogurt Conditioner

It works the same way as the mayonnaise conditioner.

Apply to your hair and rinse well.

Deep Repair Conditioner

This recipe can also act as a mask if you leave it on longer than the recipe indicates. This conditioner is best suited for damaged hair.

Mix ½ cup of jojoba oil combined with ½ cup of grape seed oil. Warm the oil mixture in a pan on low heat. Remove from heat source and add 1 tsp. of aloe vera gel and 8 drops of rosemary essential oil. Apply throughout your hair. Keep the conditioner on for 10 to 20 minutes. Rinse well.

Rinses and Hair Styling Products

Rinses, better known as leave-in conditioners in North America, are a lost art. French women don't forget this step, as it's a beauty secret they've learned from their mothers.

You need to take time for the ritual of rinsing. This step is necessary to get gorgeous hair without spending too much on styling products. You might not need to style your hair at all with a proper rinse. It removes all residues and gives an incredible shine.

Caution: if your hair is very dry and damaged due to coloring it, this could be drying.

Vinegar Rinse

Add 3 tbsp. of vinegar to a spray bottle. Fill the rest with water. Distribute the product. No need to rinse. Don't worry, the smell will not last. Use apple cider vinegar for dark hair, wine vinegar for red hair, white vinegar for blond hair.

Herbal Rinse

This rinse, made from herbs, has the same effectiveness as the vinegar rinse. It leaves hair shiny and soft.

Make an herbal tea of your choice. Use chamomile for blonde hair, rosemary and sage for darker hair. Let the tea cool down and place it in a spray bottle. Distribute the product. No need to rinse. You can also add lemon juice for oily hair.

Honey Rinse

You're probably thinking this product will make your hair sticky, but that's not the case. This recipe will help you manage frizzy hair.

Just add 1 tsp. of honey to your rinse water. Rinse one more time with clear water afterwards.

Did you know? Lemon juice is an old-fashioned way to give a shine boost to your hair, especially for oily hair.

Orange or Lemon Styling Spray

This spray will hold your hair in place. You can keep it for a few days. Choose your citrus based on your hair needs. For oily or light hair use lemon while normal, dry, and dark hair types should use orange. This recipe is still used in France by the older generation; however, even young people are beginning to use it as a natural alternative to regular hair spray.

You will need 1 lemon or orange, distilled water, and sugar. Add 1 lemon or orange (in small pieces with the peels) in 2 cups of distilled water. Bring to boil over medium heat. When half of the water has evaporated, remove your pan from the heat. Strain and add 2 to 4 tbsp. of sugar (adding a little more sugar increases the holding power). When the mixture is cool, you can add 8 drops of lavender essential oil. Pour the liquid into a spray bottle and store it in the refrigerator.

Sugar Spray

Gives extra hold, shine and body to your hair. If you spray it just at the roots of your hair and style it afterwards, it will give you even more volume.

Dissolve 1 tsp. of granulated sugar into 1 cup of distilled water. Add 3 or 4 drops of your favorite essential oil. Pour the mixture into a spray bottle. Shake well. Spray and let dry.

Coconut Spray

This spray works well on coarse hair. It gives body and texture, especially if you use the blow dryer for styling. This is often used by Tahitian women (and French women dreaming of an exotic vacation).

Pour coconut milk into a spray bottle. Spray on clean wet hair.

Hair Color

If you want to cover your grey or white hair: you use hair dye. If you want to change your look (and mood) by switching to another hair color, you use hair dye. But do you really know what's in your hair dye?

Drugstores and often hair salon dyes contain petroleum-based chemicals such as coal tar, ammonia, and phenylenediamine. In many international studies, this has caused cancer in animals. A Harvard study also declared that women who dye their hair several times a year have seventy percent increased risk for ovarian cancer.

You can use henna (look online for proper use) or rinses that will enhance your hair color. Rinses made of cranberry juice are suitable for red hair, chamomile for blond hair, coffee and cinnamon for dark hair.

The best choice is choosing a natural hair dye. Take your time and read the label. Your health comes first.

I found one brand that has the best reviews called Sanotint, which is made of millet and other natural ingredients (you can order Sanotint hair dye at www.vivasanusa.com). My hair looks even healthier with every use.

Nails

Your nails are indicative of your overall health. Whether you need to strengthen your nails or improve your cuticles, there is a solution, through the use of food.

Treat your nails in a proper way: wear gloves for gardening and washing the dishes!

A puree of kiwi, pineapple, or papaya (these are rich in enzymes) will help your nails get stronger. This will also work well on your cuticles too. If you need to lighten your nails, you can rub them with half of a lemon.

You can choose very simple products right from your kitchen to soften your cuticles and fortify your nails. Just soak your fingers in warm olive oil. Add 2 or 3 drops of lemon essential oil for a lightening effect. Do this regularly and see the results! I have seen French women using these treatments instead of getting French manicures.

Did you know? Most nail polishes and nail polish removers are made of harsh chemicals. If you check the *Suzuki Foundation* website in the *Resources* section, you will find out about the ingredients that are in this little colored bottle. It's not pretty!

There are studies that denounce all the toxins that might be absorbed through your nails, but remember nails are porous.

An array of chemicals can be found in nail polish and nail polish remover. In order to give you an idea, here is the "toxic trio": formaldehyde is a chemical causing asthma and skin irritations. Toluene, a solvent derived from petroleum, can cause skin irritation and respiratory problems. Dibutyl phthalate (DBP) is a plasticizer and seems to find its way through the nails up to the body's fatty tissues. It may create hormonal imbalances and other serious issues such as miscarriage (in animal tests).

Many studies denounce that both nail polish and nail polish remover may have their fair share of harmful ingredients for our health...

Do you like the smell of nail polish remover? I know I don't. Now that I don't use it, I no longer experience headaches. Nail polish remover contains acetone and toluene. Some nail polish removers claim to be acetone free, but they have ethyl acetate instead. A lovely chemical cocktail with shady ingredients that are highly flammable!

You can find natural brands of nail polishes that are safe to use. I found one at www.acquarella.com, a site that sells water-based nail polishes. These polishes eventually peel off after a while or you can purchase their safe nail polish remover. You can look on *EWG* (skin-deep data base website mentioned in the *Resources* section) and choose other beautiful nontoxic brands too.

Alternatively, you have another option: go natural! Just polish your nails with a chamois buffer for a lovely and safe sheen.

NATURAL SOLUTIONS FOR BEAUTY PROBLEMS

This section is specifically designed to target external problems with appearance, which are often hard to get rid of. Discover natural solutions that will eliminate everything from acne to varicose veins.

These recipes will be even more effective in conjunction with good diet.

Acne

This skin condition affects girls and boys around puberty because of the hormonal changes that are taking place. Sometimes, acne lasts longer even into adulthood, and this can be a nightmare!

If you suffer from acne, it can be beneficial to investigate what's causing your acne. Your doctor or dermatologist can help narrow the search. Some possible causes include: hormone imbalance such as PCOS (polycystic ovarian syndrome), allergy, candida overgrowth, genetic factors, poor nutrition, and stress. Ask for blood tests, a hormonal panel, and a hepatic blood test.

A healthy diet can give you the key to eliminate these ugly pimples as mentioned in the section *Nutrition Tips to Fight Acne and Oily Skin*. If you've already begun this program, hopefully you're seeing a reduction in pimples. Some acne sufferers experience a change in their skin after altering their diet. This often entails reducing their sugar and sometimes gluten intake, and increasing their intake of fresh veggies and fruit. I recommend again *The Clear*

Skin Diet by Alan C. Logan: it is a wonderful book that explores the subject further.

I am an acne survivor. Thanks to a targeted, delicious, nutritious diet, as well as wonderful homemade beauty recipes, my skin is finally pimple free! I don't worry if I get an occasional zit, because I have the solution to get rid of it in the blink of an eye. I waited so long to get a clear complexion (with few wrinkles). I still can't believe it; the answer was right there in my kitchen!

Tips:

- Wash your pillowcase regularly to avoid bacterial contamination.

- Don't wear too much makeup; go bare whenever you can!

- Practice sports, fitness, and/or yoga, which will help you detoxify through sweating.

- Wash your face after your sport activities.

Choose any of the following recipes or alternate with other recipes. If you have any reaction or if you don't see any improvement after three weeks (the necessary time for the skin to adapt), change and find the right recipe for you.

SOS Solutions to Apply on Pimples

Here are the best natural emergency acne fighters to apply to inflamed areas:

- 1/2 tsp. of cinnamon powder mixed with honey *SUGAR ?*

- Honey by itself *SUGAR ?*

- Tea tree essential oil *?*

- Fresh garlic

- A few drops of lemon juice

Acne Cleanser with Oil (OCM)

As we saw in the beginning of this chapter, the oil cleansing method is very effective for acne. What? Oil for oily and acne-prone skin? Yes! Using oil is the best way to remove makeup and dirt. If you don't wear makeup, you might choose another cleanser. Cleansing your face with oil will not give you more pimples.

Choose the right oil such as jojoba, hazelnut oil, or sweet almond oil. Follow the steps carefully as explained earlier in Chapter 2, section *Makeup Removers and Cleansers*.

Aloe Vera Gel Cleanser

You might prefer to use this cleanser in combination with water-based cleansers.

Fill an old sterilized cream jar (3 ounces) with aloe vera gel. Add 3 to 6 drops of tea tree essential oil (depending on the therapeutic strength you desire). Mix well. Massage it on your face (avoid eye area). Remove it with a tissue. Follow with one of the following cleansers.

Honey Cleanser

Simply the best. The antibacterial and moisturizing properties of honey will eliminate your pimples.

Wet your face with filtered water (chlorinated water is not ideal). Use a tiny amount of honey and massage it onto wet skin. Leave it on for a few minutes if you have time. Rinse well with lukewarm water. Your skin will not be sticky, but radiant and supple.

Oat Cleanser

If you wear makeup, you skin should be clean and makeup free before using this cleanser. If you don't wear any makeup, proceed directly with this great cleanser. It is mild enough for everyday use or you can alternate with honey cleanser.

Use 1 tbsp. of powdered oats. These need to be prepared ahead of time and stored in a glass jar for daily use. Wet your skin. Wet the oats in the palm of your hand. Massage them into your skin. Rinse well.

Did you know? You can also use fresh tomato juice to clean your face. Fresh tomato juice (from a juicer) is the one I'm talking about, not the kind found at the supermarket. Mix filtered water and tomato juice. Wash you face with it. Rinse with lukewarm water.

Apple Cider Vinegar Toner

You can't miss this step. This is a very well-known toner used by French women. It is so refreshing, and it minimizes pores.

Mix ½ cup of distilled water with 1 tbsp. of apple cider vinegar. Pour it into a spray bottle or a regular bottle. Apply the toner to your skin by spraying or using a cotton ball to dab. Don't rub the toner into your skin, as rubbing will further irritate acne. Store in the refrigerator for 2 weeks.

Witch Hazel Toner

Buy the best natural witch hazel in your local health food stores. It is a traditional toner in France for acne-prone skin.

Once you've bought your witch hazel, add 8 drops of lavender essential oil or 5 drops of tea tree essential oil for more effectiveness.

Parsley Toner

Gentle toner for inflamed acne-prone skin. It is an ancestral recipe in France.

Add 1 bunch of fresh parsley to warm water. Boil for 15 minutes. Filter and cool. Keep in the refrigerator up to 2 weeks. *Caution*: this product causes photosensitivity. Do not use it if you go out in the sun.

Cucumber Toner

A true friend for acne-prone skin.

Mix the juice of 1 cucumber with 2 tbsp. of aloe vera gel. Pour it in a bottle or jar. Close it tightly. Keep it in the refrigerator for up to 5 days.

[handwritten: ① "A POT" NATURAL WATER ONLY]

Tip: for deeper cleansing, don't forget to try facial steams, masks, and gentle exfoliations on a regular basis. If your acne is very inflamed, skip the facial steams.

Apple Cider Vinegar Facial Steam *[handwritten: YES ②]*

Pour hot water in a large bowl. Add 3 tbsp. of apple cider vinegar and some rose petals (for a special touch). Proceed as usual for a facial steam.

Himalayan Salt Facial Steam *[handwritten: YES ③]*

Use 1 tsp. of Himalayan salt and proceed as usual for facial steaming.

Essential Oil Facial Steam *[handwritten: MAYBE]*

Pour 4 drops of lavender essential oil in a bowl of hot water and proceed as usual for facial steaming.

Cabbage & Tomato Facial Steam *[handwritten: MAYBE]*

The smell is not the best, but this recipe is wonderful for acne-prone skin.

You'll need to cook half of a cabbage in boiling water. You're after the broth, but you can eat the cabbage as a snack or incorporate it into a meal. Mix 50/50 with fresh tomato juice. Proceed as usual for facial steaming.

Lettuce Mask MAYBE

Yes, eat your salad and apply it to your face too!

Place 2 or 3 lettuce leaves in mineral water for a few minutes. Apply them to your skin and relax for 30 minutes. Rinse well.

Carrot Mask ?

Puree 1 steamed carrot. Mix it with 1 egg white and 3 tbsp. of yogurt. Apply to your skin and keep the mask for 30 minutes. Rinse well.

Strawberry Mask ?

You can also use papaya or mango for this one. Don't use this recipe if you have sensitive skin.

Puree the fruit and apply to your face. Keep the mask in place with gauze as needed. Leave the mask on for 15 minutes and rinse.

Egg White Mask ?

Purifies and firms your skin at the same time. This recipe is great for skin that is both mature and acne-prone.

Mix 1 egg white with 1 tsp. of lemon juice. Apply and leave on until dry. Rinse well.

Green Clay Mask YES

A <u>French classic</u>. Adding oil makes it gentle for acne-prone skin without stripping your skin's moisture.

Mix 1 tbsp. of green clay with 1 tbsp. of green tea. Add 1 tbsp. of olive oil or jojoba oil. Apply this paste on your skin and allow the mask to dry. Rinse well.

Honey & Oats Mask ?

Here again, you have two amazing acne fighting ingredients combined for the best result!

Mix 3 tbsp. of powdered oats with 2 tsp. of honey. Add milk or yogurt to create a paste. Apply and leave on for 20 minutes. Rinse well.

Moisturizing Mask MAYBE

Acne-prone skin occasionally needs a moisturizing mask to calm down inflammation and soften irritated areas.

Mix 2 tbsp. of flour with 2 tbsp. of jojoba oil. Add 1 tsp. of milk. Mix well. Apply and leave on for 20 minutes. Rinse well.

Acne-prone skin is not easy to treat; choose your moisturizer well:

Floral Mist

This is an alternative way to moisturize acne-prone skin.

Mix equal parts witch hazel and rose water. Put the mixture in a spray bottle.

Acne Serum TOO COMPLICATED

This serum is lightweight, making it very suitable for acne-prone skin. At times, creams can be too rich and can leave the skin too shiny.

Mix ½ cup of hazelnut oil with 1 ½ tbsp. of apricot kernel oil. Add 6 drops of tea tree essential oil and 6 drops of rosemary essential oil. Pour the mixture into an old sterilized cream jar. This serum keeps well in the refrigerator for several months.

Aloe Vera Serum ? MAYBE TOO MANY INGREDIENTS

My mother always has aloe vera gel in her home. I began to create this serum when I couldn't find one suited to my skin. It is a perfect anti-shine serum.

Mix 1 ½ tbsp. of aloe vera gel with 1 tsp. of hazelnut oil. Add 5 drops of tea tree essential oil and 4 drops of lavender essential oil. Mix well. Optional: add 2 drops of rosehip oil for an extra vitamin C boost.

Aloe Vera & Rosehip Serum YES

This is a variation of the aloe vera serum that provides anti-aging benefits.

With a small whisk, mix well 1 tsp. of aloe vera gel with 3 drops of tea tree essential oil, and 3 drops of rosehip oil. Place it in an old sterilized cream jar.

Moisturizer for Adult Acne

Taking care of acne and wrinkles is not always easy. This recipe handles both concerns.

Mix 2 tbsp. of jojoba oil with 1 tbsp. of apricot kernel oil (add 1 tsp. of evening primrose oil for even more anti-aging properties if desired). Add 1 drop of carrot essential oil and 2 drops of lavender essential oil. Mix well and pour the mixture in an old sterilized cream jar. Keeps well in the fridge for several weeks.

Black Heads

Another nightmare, but don't worry! Food-based DIY recipes will solve your problems.

Black heads are pimples that are not covered by skin and become black due to oxidation. All the recipes pertaining to black heads are best to be used after a facial steam or a purifying mask.

Honey MAYBE

On clean and dry skin, apply a dollop of honey on the affected areas. Tap with your finger for 5 minutes. Rinse completely. The stickiness of the honey will suck the black heads out and leave anti-bacterial ingredients on the applied area.

Egg White

Apply 3 successive layers of 1 beaten egg white. Let each layer to dry before applying the next one. Rinse. Another solution: soak a little strip of paper towel in egg white mixture and apply on your nose or other area. Let it dry and remove it. See what's left on the strip!

Nutmeg MAYBE

Nutmeg is a go-to beauty ingredient among French women.

Mix 1 tsp. of nutmeg powder with a tiny amount of heavy cream. Rub it into the area with black heads. Rinse well.

with
CREAM

Large Pores

Egg White Mask

You won't find a better pore minimizer than this. This is the same technique as in the previous section (see egg white mask recipe for black heads). Proceed as usual. Enjoy your new complexion.

Honey Mask

Same recipe as for black heads. Just leave the mask on the face longer than for the black head removal technique. This mask is promoted in many beauty French workshops.

Almond Mask

This product has a dual function; it acts as a mask and an exfoliator.

Mix ¼ cup of almond flour with 1 ½ tbsp. of rose water. Then, add 2 tbsp. of yogurt. Apply and leave on for 15 minutes. Massage your skin thoroughly before rinsing.

Tomato Mask

Puree 1 tomato and apply on your skin. Put a light cloth over your face to keep it in place. Enjoy!

Toner

Both witch hazel and cucumber juice are great pore minimizers.

Brown Spots (or Age Spots)

Brown spots usually appear on the skin after years of sun exposure. Studies say they can also occur because of vitamin deficiencies, poor nutrition, excess of sugar, alcohol, and smoking.

 Drink lemon water to detoxify and try one of the following recipes:

Facial Brown Spots

Apply a mask of plain organic unsweetened yogurt 2 times a week. Keep on for 20 minutes and rinse well.

Brown Spots on the Hands

Puree half of a ripe papaya and mix it with 1 tbsp. of lemon and 1 tsp. of honey. Apply it on affected area. Keep on for 5 minutes and rinse well. Massage your hands with the oil recipe below (prepare oil recipe in advance).

Anti-Brown Spots Oil TRY

This recipe comes straight out of my grandmother's notebook.

Soak ¼ cup of fresh dandelion leaves in 4 tbsp. of castor oil and pour it in a glass bottle with a tight lid. Let it rest for 3 weeks. Apply this oil daily on your hands.

Dry Hands OR FEET TO TRY

Prevention first! Wear gloves when working in your garden, cleaning dishes, or going outside in winter. Need a simple solution? Exfoliate your hands with powdered oats mixed with honey.

Here are more ideas...

Another deep moisturizing treatment can be made when you combine half of a ripe avocado in a blender with 1 tsp. of avocado oil. Massage your hands. Wear cotton gloves and keep this hand mask overnight. My mum has the softest hands in the world. I know her secret!

If your hands are damaged, massage them every night with a mixture of 1 tbsp. of olive oil and 1 tbsp. of honey. Once again, wear cotton gloves and keep the mixture overnight.

Nail Fungus

Nails will turn yellow or brown due to a fungal infection. To get rid of the infection, your nails should be treated on regular basis.

Apply a small amount of pureed garlic on the affected area (not on the skin) and put a Band-Aid over it. Tea tree essential oil applied topically is very effective too.

Brittle Nails

First find the cause of this condition. Some possibilities include systemic issues or use of chlorinated water or chemical products.

The best recipe is simple: rub your finger in a half lemon. That's it!

Nail Strengthening Oil

Mix 1 tsp. of castor oil with 1 tsp. of sweet almond oil. Optional: add ¼ tsp. of liquid vitamin E. Apply this oil mixture each night before going to bed.

Scars

I used this one on my scars after a terrible ski accident. It's an ancestral remedy in France for healing scars. It worked so well!

When the scar is closed, apply aloe vera gel or honey. You should massage your scar with avocado oil or rosehip oil too. It will regenerate the skin and minimize dryness.

Stretch Marks

This is a recipe that French mothers pass onto their daughters.

Combine 2 tbsp. of sweet almond oil with ½ tsp. of coconut oil. Add 1 drop of liquid Vitamin E and 3 drops of lavender essential oil. Mix well. Massage the area every day. Wheat germ oil, by itself, is also very effective.

Psoriasis and Eczema

Speak to your doctor about these conditions.

Apply raw potato juice (use a juicer) or borage seed oil. Always do a skin test before or discontinue if any reaction occurs.

Varicose Veins

This problem is more internal than external. Varicose veins have several causes: too much sun exposure, extreme heat (prolonged Jacuzzi use), standing for long periods of time, genetic factors, and smoking.

Here are some solutions...

Tip: do not cross your legs when sitting! Instead, try to elevate them as much as possible.

You will find relief with one of these DIY recipes:

- Apply a mixture of fresh cabbage leaves (only the tender part) and 2 tbsp. of olive oil onto the affected area. Put a loose bandage around and keep it on for 30 minutes. Repeat this treatment 3 times per week.

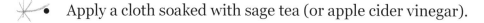

- Apply a cloth soaked with sage tea (or apple cider vinegar).

- Many people have great results by gently applying a mixture of ¼ cup coconut oil and 30 drops of rosemary essential oil to the affected area.

Puffy Eyes

There are many causes for puffy eyes: allergic reactions, excessive consumption of alcohol, drugs, and sugar.

Food-based recipes to relieve puffy eyes are amazing! Apply on your eyes and relax. Make your choice from below:

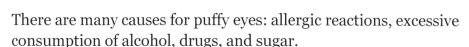

- 2 cold tea bags of chamomile tea (but it's better to soak 2 cotton balls in a homemade chamomile tea). They should be chilled in the refrigerator for a few minutes.

- 2 slices of cucumber (a classic).

- 2 cotton balls soaked in fresh milk.

- 2 slices of potato (or melon).

Dark Circles

We've all had a night where we didn't get enough sleep. In the morning, you're greeted with dark circles under your eyes. Other causes for dark circles include allergy, hereditary factors, loss of collagen due to aging, and too many hours in front of the computer.

Don't fret, below are a few ways you can keep dark circles under wraps:

- Pat a small amount of grated raw potato under your eyes. Lay down and relax. Leave it on for 5 minutes.

- Do an under-eye mask with sweet almond oil and honey a few times a week. Sweet almond oil is known for its lightening properties. Leave it on for 5 minutes. Rinse.

- Another under-eye mask to fight dark circles: mix equal proportion of potato juice and cucumber juice. Add 1 tsp. of honey and apply. Leave it on for 5 minutes. Rinse.

- At night, try Michel Phan gel recipe (I came across Michel on YouTube). Mix 2 drops of licorice extract (lightening agent) with 3 drops of vitamin K (from a gel capsule) and 1 drop of aloe vera gel. Mix well. Pour this gel into a small and sterilized container. Apply at night.

Cellulite

Who doesn't have cellulite? Please, raise your hand! Thin women have it. Young women have it. You are not alone! The causes are multiple: genetic factors, poor diet, poor bad blood circulation, age, and sedentary lifestyle.

Tip: follow the Beautifying Diet described in the first chapter.

Enjoy these great anti-cellulite recipes. After the scrubs, you can massage the affected areas with macadamia oil lotion.

Coffee Scrub

French women use this scrub to prepare their skin a few months before summer. They're already thinking of which swimsuit they will wear at the beach. It's great motivation! Drinking your coffee will not help to get rid of your cellulite. Instead, use it topically.

During the month before summer, exfoliate the affected area with 4 tbsp. of coffee ground mixed with 1 ½ tbsp. of honey. Massage well and rinse. Moisturize after with macadamia oil (see the macadamia oil recipe below).

Fruit Scrub

Massage a puree of kiwi or pineapple into the affected area (and eat it too, of course). Alternate this fruity massage with a massage of coconut oil. You will feel like you are at the beach!

Olive Oil & Salt Scrub

Mix ¼ cup of olive oil with the same amount of sea salt. Add 4 drops of lavender essential oil. Massage into the affected area. Rinse well. Apply macadamia oil.

Macadamia Oil

Here is the famous macadamia oil treatment.

Mix 4 tbsp. of macadamia oil with 5 drops of grapefruit essential oil. For extra strength, you might add 1 tsp. of seaweed powder.

Seaweed Wrap

A great detoxifying product that is so effective for cellulite! This is a typical French homemade body treatment. To get in the mood you can light candles, play soft music, and make a cup of herbal tea.

Mix 1 cup of kelp powder with 1 cup of hot water. Add the water gradually. Sit in your dry bathtub, sofa, or an area of floor covered with large towels. Apply the mixture to your thighs and other affected areas. The mixture should adhere to your skin easily. Then, wrap these areas with sheets of plastic and cover yourself with large towels to hold in your body heat. Sit like this for 20 minutes. Remove the plastic wrap and towels. You can either soak in your bathtub for 10 minutes or rinse off in your shower. Taking a seaweed bath or herbal bath will finalize the treatment.

Cottage Cheese Wrap

This is one of the recipes that I learnt in a beauty workshop in France.

Mix together 2 parts cottage cheese with 1 part coffee grounds. Put a bath towel on your sofa. Lay down and apply the mixture on the affected area. Cover it with the plastic wrap. Relax. Leave the treatment on for 30 minutes and rinse well. Then, apply in circular motions your DIY macadamia oil.

Hair Loss

Men and women suffer from hair loss (this section is not about seasonal hair loss which is temporary). Stress, hereditary factors, poor nutrition, poor blood circulation, and reaction to chemical products can all cause hair loss. You'll have to determine if you still have healthy hair roots or not. Scalp massage is a solution that stimulates blood circulation. These recipes work for some and not for others, depending on a multitude of factors. Stick with it for at least 3 months. In case of severe hair loss, you might consider taking natural supplements with the help of your naturopath in addition to a healthy diet.

Hair & Scalp Tonic

This tonic recipe was presented in many workshops I attended in Europe.

Mix 1 cup of distilled water with 1 cup of aloe vera juice and 1 cup of a fresh stinging nettles herbal tea at room temperature. Add 12 drops of rosemary essential oil and 14 drops of sage essential oil. Massage thoroughly into the scalp and leave on at least 30 minutes. Repeat every night if possible.

Castor Oil Mask

Mix 1 tbsp. of castor oil and 1 tbsp. of coconut oil. Add 5 drops of rosemary essential oil. Massage the mixture thoroughly into the scalp and leave it on overnight wearing a shower cap (I know, not very romantic). Shampoo in the morning with a homemade shampoo that uses 1 or 2 drops of the following essential oils: thyme, sage, rosemary, or eucalyptus. Repeat this process several times a week.

Onion Mask

Juice 1 fresh onion with a juicer. Mix the juice with equal parts of castor oil. I recommend adding a few drops of lemon essential oil to help mask the smell. Massage it thoroughly into the scalp and wear a shower cap. Cover the shower cap with a warm towel (keep this mask on overnight if possible). Shampoo and rinse well in the morning. Use it for 2 weeks or alternate with the previous mask. Then stop for 2 weeks and use it again.

CHAPTER 3

Easy Homemade Beauty Food Makeup Recipes

You now know that a beauty food diet is the first step to your true natural beauty. You have also discovered how beauty foods allow you to create DIY beauty recipes that enhance your beauty day after day at low cost and without chemicals.

Why not pursue an adventure with beauty food makeup?

You're probably wondering why formulating your own makeup, when you can choose from numerous commercial brands? We've talked about beauty care products (shampoo, face cream, body lotion). Many international studies denounce all the chemical ingredients hidden in makeup too. Go online and look at the Suzuki foundation website or read this famous book *Drop Dead Gorgeous* by Kim Erickson. It will give you an idea of what really is in your lipstick and your foundation.

I discovered *Drop Dead Gorgeous* when I was trying to eliminate toxins from my body to be healthier. It was a wakeup call! I was horrified: my lipstick had lead in it, my cream foundation contained propylene glycol, and my mascara relied on parabens preservatives for a longer shelf life. I couldn't believe how many artificial chemicals I was ingesting daily. I decided to find another solution.

If you still want to buy regular makeup over-the-counter, check the skin-deep data base (www.ewg.org/skindeep) to find a natural or organic one. Have a look at another great website to be informed about the potentially dangerous toxins found in cosmetics: www.safecosmetics.org.

The other solution is to create your own makeup line. Don't be discouraged; it is possible! Get ready to use your beauty food to create your own natural cosmetics.

You will be blown away by the results!

Many simple recipes and techniques can help you to look gorgeous with fruity, colorful, and pure makeup. The bonus? Your skin receives one hundred percent of the active ingredients. You will improve your skin while looking great!

The actual trend is to go all natural. Look at the green celebrity's endorsements, books, and websites about it. Embrace this movement and enjoy it to the fullest. Come back to the old-fashioned way that ensures your makeup is kind to you and to the planet! When you use your own makeup, it means less packaging and less toxic load polluting the earth.

It is not a new hip idea; it is a return to real beauty. In fact, this new approach comes from ancient history, when women used grapes to tint their lips and cheeks (they mixed it into a cream).

In the past, women didn't have access to information about the ingredients they were using. But nowadays, we are lucky; we can do our own research. So, check out reputable websites about toxicity in cosmetics. It's worth it: you deserve to be informed and make decisions accordingly.

So, let's go and apply what's on your plate to your face! Learn the benefits of food-based and raw makeup. Ever since I used these recipes, I've been crazy about them. Not only do natural products enhance your beauty, but they contribute to your sense of well-being and happiness. Knowing you are using all-natural ingredients is so satisfying! You will be proud to say to your friends and family members: "*I am beautiful naturally*"!

French women are addicted to their makeup and don't like to step out of their home bare faced. There are two types of French women: the ones who are very sophisticated, wearing makeup from morning to night (real makeup junkies) and the second type who are minimalists. The minimalist category of women loves to be effortlessly beautiful. It often looks like they have no makeup on, but in fact, they use makeup: their own homemade makeup mixtures made from simple ingredients.

The trend of DIY makeup is growing more and more in Europe. You can find beauty workshops in Paris or other cities (such as the one I attended to learn how to use our daily food as beautifying ingredients). Why not create your own workshop on the weekend, and have fun with friends making your own cosmetics?

So, let's start right away!

Caution: all these DIY makeup recipes have been tested and approved by myself and many other users. I'm not a biochemist. These recipes are based on reliable information. Use these recipes with caution and at your own risk.

Always test the final product on the inner portion of your arm, wait forty-eight hours and check for any allergic reactions. You need to be meticulous about hygiene when making your own makeup to avoid bacterial growth. Wash your hands carefully before beginning any recipe. Sterilize all your tools (whisk, spoon, measure cup, syringe, and containers that you will store your makeup in) by putting them in boiling water (a complete sterilization takes 20 minutes). Dry your tools with a clean towel. For your makeup, you can use old containers (clean and sterilized) or buy new ones on line.

Now, enjoy being beautified by food!

MAKEUP FOR ONE TIME USE ONLY

Because you use fresh ingredients, these recipes are for immediate use only.

Discover now the beauty of raw makeup!

Clear Mascara

Use a well cleaned old mascara wand. This product does not give any color, but it will separate your lashes. After your lashes have dried they will have a sheen and definition.

Use one egg white (organic if possible). Dip the wand into the egg white mixture and apply it as you would do with regular mascara.

Tinted Mascara

Activated charcoal is what gives this black mascara its color. You can buy activated charcoal in health food stores. Don't worry it's not the same charcoal that you use for your barbecue!

In a little cup, mix a tiny amount of aloe vera gel with raw unsweetened cocoa powder (brown tint) or activated charcoal (black tint). Dip a clean mascara wand into the mixture and apply it as usual. If you have long eyelashes, try the coconut mascara described later.

Eye Liner

For a primer, apply a small amount of oil around your eyes (choose an oil that best suits your skin type). This will ensure that the eye liner glides on and stays in place.

Place a small amount in a bowl of raw unsweetened cocoa powder (for brown shade) or a tiny pinch of activated charcoal powder (one capsule of activated charcoal for black tint). Dip an eyeliner brush (the tiniest possible) into the mixture. Apply it the same way as regular eyeliner.

Mattifying Potato

Potato as makeup? Sound strange, but potato will help keep your makeup fresh. When I was young, I saw women using it, and I still can't believe how effective it is!

Cut a potato into two pieces. Dab the cut side over your freshly made-up face or bare skin. It fixes your makeup and acts as an anti-shine powder.

Quick Loose Powder

The best part of this recipe is how quickly it can be made; it just takes one minute!

Arrowroot powder is the base of this recipe. To better match your skin tone, you'll have to add a tinting agent. For fair to medium tones, you can add a tiny amount of cinnamon or ginger powder. For medium to darker tones, add a small amount of nutmeg powder and raw cocoa powder. Play and find your color. You are the artist of your beauty!

Eyebrow Tint

This old technique has been used for years in Europe and is making a come-back due to all-natural makeup trends. This is a favorite recipe of beauty workshops and a great example of raw makeup.

With an eyebrow brush, apply a tiny amount of raw unsweetened cocoa or activated charcoal or even blackberry puree to fill in your eyebrow. Fix it with the honey eyebrow gel (see section *Makeup for Multiple Uses* for this recipe*)*.

Red Beet Cheeks and Lip Tint

This is *the* recipe that sparked my interest in edible and food-based makeup. I learned it in a beauty workshop in France and now I can't live without it! This product melts into your skin and is incredibly long lasting.

Take a fresh red beet (organic if possible, no need to put pesticide on your face) and cut a small disc. Store the rest of the red beet in a plastic bag in the refrigerator. Apply it on your cheeks and/or lips, and blend the color and coverage to your liking. Add 1 or 2 drops of grape seed oil to your cheeks as a natural highlighter.

Fruity Lipstick

Beauty food is the answer when you want to tint your lips with vivid colors! Nature offers all the shades of tint you desire. In the past, before modern lipsticks existed, French women and other women in the world tinted their lips and cheeks this way.

Choose a fruit based on the color you desire: raspberry (light rose), cranberry (bright red), pomegranate (rosy red), black cherry (dark red), red grape (purple red), and blackberry (dark mauve). You can mix two or more fruit to create a hybrid color. Make a fruit puree, and use a cotton tip or a tiny brush (clean it between each use) to apply to your lips. For extra shine, add a touch of grape seed oil or liquid vitamin E.

MAKEUP FOR MULTIPLE USES

These next recipes are very simple. If you want your products to have longer shelf life, you might decide to follow makeup recipes that use natural preservatives.

For information about more elaborate recipes, look for books and websites about natural homemade makeup in the section *Resources*.

Coconut Mascara

The beauty instructor at a workshop in the south of France used this mascara on her lashes and it convinced me to use it too. It has a longer shelf life than the previous recipe while giving color and definition to your eyelashes. Coconut is a great base as it has antibacterial properties. If at any point, you smell a fishy odor, discard it and make a fresh one.

Use an old but clean mascara container. To determine the proper amount for your container, first fill it with water. Pour the water into a small measuring cup, and you will see the amount of coconut oil to use. Place that amount of coconut oil into a small bowl, and mix in a pinch of raw cocoa powder (brown) or activated charcoal powder (black) until you have the color you desire. Use a small syringe (without the needle) to suck the mixture from the bowl and add it to the mascara container. It can be kept for several days in the refrigerator. Warm it in your hands before each use.

Aloe Vera & Coconut Mascara

This mascara contains beeswax that will allow you to keep it one to four months. No mascara should be used longer than that to avoid bacterial growth.

Mix 2 tsp. of coconut oil, 4 tsp. of aloe vera gel, and ½ tsp. of beeswax in a small saucepan. Warm up the ingredients until beeswax is dissolved. When the mixture cools, add a pinch of raw cocoa powder or activated charcoal powder (1 or 2 capsules). Mix well. Proceed the same way as for the coconut mascara recipe.

Honey Eyebrow Gel

This recipe is so simple; you'll ask yourself why you have not used it before. Honey has great anti-bacterial properties, which contribute to its long shelf life. Get sweet eyebrows and thank bees for this recipe!

You'll need liquid raw honey. Use a syringe (without the needle) to suck the honey and place it into a sterilized old mascara container. Apply as usual.

Loose Powder/Bronzer

You can use arrow root or potato starch as base for powders and bronzers (and put the mixture in an old sterilized powder container). Prepare powders in small batches to avoid spoiling or bacteria growth.

Put arrowroot or potato starch in a small bowl. Mix in a pinch of kaolin clay (perfect for normal to combination skin). You can add raw cocoa powder or carob powder for a tawny shade, adding cinnamon will create bronze shade. Add a few drops of grapefruit seed extract as a natural preservative. A friend of mine uses turmeric to calm down redness, but use it sparingly and be aware of its staining power.

Eye Shadow

Apply a touch of sweet almond oil on your eyelid before applying your food-based eye shadow. It will help the eye shadow adhere, acting like a primer.

Using a Q-tip, makeup brushes, or your fingers, apply your favorite shade of eye shadow: powdered spirulina for green color, powdered walnut shell for brown, and cornstarch mixed with dehydrated red beet powder for rose. You can also create hybrid shades by mixing two or more of the coloring agents.

Red Beet Powdered Blush

Red beet is truly a versatile product. Dried red beetroot powder can be made easily in a blender from dehydrated red beet slices or purchased at your local health food store. With a food dehydrator, you can create various shades of red from strawberries and raspberries. This appliance is also useful for making healthy snacks like dried fruit and veggie chips.

Pour red beet powder or other fruit powder (even hibiscus flower powder) in an old sterilized loose powder container. Use a brush to apply it to your cheeks.

Lip Balm

This is the easiest elaborate makeup product you can create. This balm is moisturizing and very helpful for dry cracked lips, especially in the winter. The beauty instructor showed me a basic lip balm that had a mild scent thanks to lavender essential oil. Amazingly simple and so soft on my lips!

Melt ½ oz. of grated beeswax on very low heat in a double boiler. Stir until the wax liquefies. Then stir in 1 tsp. of honey and let the mixture cool. Add 1 drop of vitamin E and the essential oil of your choice (lavender, lemon, or peppermint). Stir well. If the mixture is too runny, add more beeswax. If it is too hard, add 1 or 2 drops of liquid Vitamin E. If you desire a shimmer in your lip balm, add mica powder. Pour the mixture quickly into a small sterilized container with a tightly sealed lid. Let the lip balm cool until firm. You can keep it up to 3 months. Don't expose this lip balm to sunlight or high temperature as it will melt! Discard it if the consistency changes.

CONCLUSION

Now you have the knowledge to maximize your beauty and health with the help of food. When you walk into a grocery store and see fruit and vegetables, you'll know these are not just items of produce, but tools of nourishment for your internal and external health. Think of your grocery list as your beauty list.

By creating a tailored beauty routine for yourself with natural products, you'll save money. Plus, you will eliminate your intake of toxins and avoid synthetic components (found in store bought cosmetics).

Beauty doesn't solely come from taking care of yourself physically. Live life to the fullest and adopt a positive attitude. Be happy! This will ensure that you are gorgeous from the inside out!

Become your own beauty planner.

Look fabulous with beauty food!

SMART AND SAFE ORGANIC MAKEUP SHOPPING

Some of you will be so pleased with your own personalized food-based makeup, that you might skip this section.

When shopping for organic makeup (think twice if you want to continue using regular commercial makeup), be smart and do your homework. If you see ingredients that you can't pronounce, run! Educate yourself. Read the labels and check for purity of the ingredients.

There are some great natural and organic brands you can trust.

Here is a list of safe cosmetic brands:

- www.drhauschka.com (wonderful organic makeup line and more)

- www.lavera.com (makeup and beauty products)

- www.100percentpure.com (wide variety of makeup)

And for the beauty of your nail and hair:

- www.acquarella.com (nontoxic nail polish)

- www.vivasanusa.com (Sanotint hair dye)

Resources

Books and eBooks

Close, Barbara. *Pure Skin Organic Beauty Basics*. Chronicle Books, 2005. This book offers great recipes with gorgeous pictures.

Erickson, Kim. *Drop-Dead Gorgeous*. Contemporary Books, 2002. I learnt about toxicity in beauty care in this book. It is extremely comprehensive on the subject.

Farrer-Halls, Gill. *Natural Beauty Recipe Book: How to Make Your Own Organic Cosmetics and Beauty Products*. Quarry Books, 2006. This is a bible about natural beauty.

Logan, Allan C. *The Clear Skin Diet*. Cumberland House, 2007. The best guide to eradicate acne through diet.

Martin, Leslie. *Crunchy Betty's Food on Your Face for Acne and Oily Skin*. Amazon, 2011.This eBook is about how to treat acne with food. It is full of amazing recipes and tips.

Mars, Brigitte. *Beauty by Nature*. Healthy Living Publication, 2006. A complete guide to true natural beauty in a gentle way.

WEBSITES

www.canadianvitaminshop.com: This wonderful company has everything (homemade beauty skin care and supplements).

www.crunchybetty.com: A wonderful eBook about nutrition and natural skin care for acne.

www.davidsuzuki.org: This is the reference to check about the chemicals in your beauty care products, plus information on how to be eco-friendly.

www.doterra.com: High quality essential oils.

www.ewg.org/skindeep: This is the data base of all beauty products.

www.health-matters.ca: Great website of Mary Jane O'Byrne who helped me to find solutions for my health and my skins issues.

www.lifestylemarkets.com: This company offers all you need to stay healthy, eat well, and find the DIY ingredients for your homemade skin care.

www.michellephan.com: Great site with amazing advice on both beauty and wellness. (Check out her videos on YouTube).

www.mountainroseherbs.com: Supplier where you can order beauty ingredients for your homemade beauty products and makeup, such as clay.

www.nezzanaturals.com: An amazing company where you can purchase all the ingredients you need for your DIY skin care.

www.safecosmetics.org: This website will help you educate yourself about toxicity in cosmetics.

www.starwest-botanicals.com: A wonderful company where you can order bulk herbs and bulk teas, such as rosehip tea.

www.wellnessmama.com: A great website with many DIY recipes from our mothers and grandmothers.

OTHER

Leon's Anti-Aging Beauty Secrets (PDF files).

Megan, Elysabeth. *Easy to Be Raw* (check out the red beet tutorial on YouTube).

Index

X

Y

Z

ABOUT THE AUTHOR

Colette Cecile was born in 1965 in Paris, France. She grew up in the countryside of central France amid organic vegetable gardens and fruit orchards. Later in life, she then moved to the beautiful French Riviera, received a master's degree in French literature and art history from the University of Nice, and became a French teacher.

Colette now lives in British Columbia, Canada. Both she and her husband also stayed in Maui, Hawaii. These two locations have had a lasting impression, inspiring Colette with their natural beauty and active lifestyles.

Health challenges motivated her to seek natural healing. Colette set out to reconnect with a family heritage, starting with healthy nutrition and plant-based beauty products described in her grandmother's journal. This book is a very personal sharing of recipes, techniques, and beauty secrets she uses in her daily life that helped her to improve her complexion (she suffered with acne and eczema for years).

When she is not on Skype connecting with her family and friends or speaking about new recipes, she likes to read, take long walks, play tennis, and create fashion accessories.

22418884R00111

Made in the USA
Columbia, SC
31 July 2018